GUIDE TO THE
Amish Country

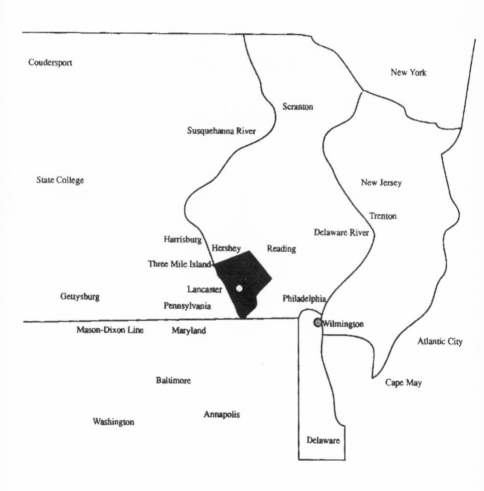

GUIDE TO THE
Amish Country

3RD EDITION

by Bill Simpson

PELICAN PUBLISHING COMPANY
Gretna 2003

First edition, August 1992
Second edition, October 1995
Third edition, April 2003

*The word "Pelican" and the depiction of a pelican are trademarks
of Pelican Publishing Company, Inc., and are registered
in the U.S. Patent and Trademark Office.*

Library of Congress Cataloging-in-Publication Data

Simpson, Bill, 1950-
    Guide to the Amish country / by Bill Simpson.— 3rd ed.
        p. cm.
Includes index.
    ISBN 1-58980-083-4 (alk. paper)
    1. Amish Country (Pa.)—Guidebooks. I. Title.
    F157.P44 S56 2003
    917.48'150444—dc21

                                                        2002153158

Printed in the United States of America

Published by Pelican Publishing Company, Inc.
1000 Burmaster Street, Gretna, Louisiana 70053

Contents

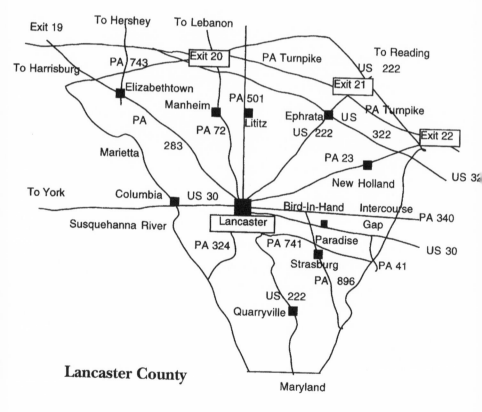

Lancaster County

Introduction

The Attraction of the Amish

In the world of tourist attractions, the Amish have a unique distinction. With the possible exception of the stars in Hollywood, the Amish are the only group of people who have become a tourist attraction. In other places, visitors come to see scenery, cities, beaches, theatres, shopping malls, amusement parks, mountains, and historical sites. In Lancaster County, visitors come to see the Amish people, and the Amish definitely aren't the stars of Hollywood.

The Amish don't dress like Hollywood stars, and they don't seek publicity. They avoid cameras because their religion teaches them that photography represents vanity. They do nothing to request attention, yet they've become a big tourist attraction. Given their choices, the Amish would choose not to be the objects of others' attention, but they're practical people, and they've learned to live with the attention and even to benefit from it.

Tourists represent a big market to which the Amish can sell their foods and other goods, which is somewhat ironic because the Amish religion forbids the acquisition of money and material, goods simply for the sake of having them or impressing one's neighbors.

So the Amish use their money to buy more farms and to

keep their families and communities together. God and family are the centers of Amish life, and it's their choice to focus on spiritual rather than material values that makes them so popular.

The attraction of the Amish lies in their strong faith, their seemingly simple lifestyles, and their selective use of much of the technology that defines life in modern America. Their lifestyle is different from the lifestyles of almost everybody else in the U.S.A., and that difference makes them interesting to other people.

Of course, it's not really accurate to say that they're completely different from other people. They dress differently and travel differently, but their goals are essentially the same as the goals of most other people: to live happily in this life and to do the same in the next life. They just happen to have chosen a road less traveled to reach their goals.

Their beliefs tell them that cars and other modern gadgets won't help them find happiness or salvation, but Amish life isn't about what they don't have. Instead, it's about what they do have. They have strong Christian faiths, strong families and communities, and their lives aren't really as simple as they may appear. The Amish still have bills and taxes to pay and families to rear, and they face the challenges of traveling in buggies in a world of fast cars and big trucks.

Amish lives still focus on God, family, and hard work, but their lives are definitely not the same as they were in the 1700s, as some writers like to romanticize. At the ends of many Amish driveways are little sheds that house telephones that they use for business. They use hospitals and doctors, and they do travel in cars, vans, buses, and trains. They just don't own cars, although even that statement comes with a caveat.

You might see a car or a pickup truck on an Amish farm, and it could belong to someone who lives there. The defining point of the Amish religion is adult baptism, so someone who has reached the legal Pennsylvania driving age of sixteen but who hasn't yet officially joined the church may own and operate a car or truck. On joining the church, however, the car must go.

The Amish are a totally religious society, but they do enjoy life. If your timing is right, you may see groups of Amish men playing softball at a park in Paradise. You'll know that it's an Amish team by the buggies around the field. On Whitmonday, fifty days after Easter, you may see the Amish playing croquet and not working at all. You may see them enjoying themselves at Dutch Wonderland Amusement Park or riding the Strasburg RailRoad. The Amish work hard and pray hard, but they also enjoy their lives.

The Amish have a powerful work ethic, and because the farm economy is volatile and often weak, almost all Amish families have cottage industries—businesses that supplement their farm incomes. The most common of these businesses are woodworking and quilt-making, but you'll also find everything from metalworking to health-food stores on Amish farms. Because farms are expensive and scarce in Lancaster County, many Amish men no longer work as farmers. Instead, many work in manufacturing and construction.

A tip on buying directly from Amish businesses: You'll save money. Whether it's a quilt, a desk, or an order from a health-food store, you'll find lower prices on the farm than in the city or at the mall. *Example:* On a Saturday afternoon at Miller's Natural Foods on Monterey Road, the small parking lot often holds license plates from many states other than Pennsylvania. The people in those cars have found that they can save enough on their purchases to justify the trip to Lancaster County, and they can always enjoy some of the other attractions while they're in town.

Plus, shopping at Miller's is a distinctly different experience from shopping at the health-food store at the mall. At Miller's, all the workers are Amish. Sometimes they speak in Pennsylvania Dutch, a regional dialect that's a mix of German and English. And you'll find some interesting items at Miller's that you won't find in suburbia, such as Amish folk remedies and advertisements for live blood testing.

At some Amish businesses, you can pay by credit card. At

Riehl's Quilts and Crafts on Eby Road, Amish women weave quilts by hand, and customers arrive by the busload and pay with MasterCard. The Amish are very practical, and if accepting credit cards helps them earn money to keep their farms and their families intact, then they'll use credit cards.

As a rule, the Amish pass their farms down through their families, but when a family has many sons and only one farm, all the sons can't work on the same land, so some must either work off the farm or move to another area.

Because of the scarcity of land, the Amish from Lancaster County have been establishing new communities for many decades, in both neighboring counties and in other states. Lancaster County was the first Amish settlement in the country, so directly or indirectly, all Amish have links to Lancaster County.

Rumors occasionally arise that, because of the suburban sprawl in Lancaster County, the Amish are thinking of leaving en masse, but those rumors aren't true for many reasons.

First, Lancaster County is home. Like everyone else, the Amish have strong ties to home, and in their close community, the ties are extremely strong.

Second, it's good dirt. The soil of Lancaster County produces much better crops than the soil almost anywhere else. The climate is relatively mild, and in most years, rainfall is adequate.

The initial attraction to Lancaster County for the Amish was the soil. It's rich, limestone soil that produces bountiful crops, and the limestone also produces another major industry: quarries. Throughout Lancaster County, quarries produce large quantities of stone for buildings, highways, and many other uses, and the county has half a dozen streets named Quarry Road.

One unusual product made from Lancaster County stone is Diamond-Tex infield mix. Used on baseball and softball fields in many states, it comes from a quarry in eastern Lancaster County.

In Lancaster County, buying farms to keep them in agriculture is difficult because farmers often find themselves bidding against real-estate developers for land. Because suburban homes generally bring higher prices than corn and soybeans, developers often have deeper pockets than farmers do. Even without competition from developers, the Amish would have trouble finding enough farms in Lancaster County, simply because all the farmland is already in use. If you see a wooded hillside in a farming area, it means that the wooded area is too steep for farming.

Because of their powerful work ethic, Lancaster County Amish are relatively prosperous, and they can afford to buy more farmland. Unlike many Americans, they don't strive to earn lots of money so that they can sit around and do nothing. To the Amish, work is its own reward. It's one of the things that God put them here to do, and they do plenty of it.

So what's the attraction?

In the hectic world of modern America, a place where people travel at twelve miles per hour in horse-drawn buggies offers an opportunity to live vicariously at a slower pace. A place where barefoot children walk to one-room schools makes it easy to fantasize about leading a more relaxed life. A place where roadside stands overflow with produce directly from the garden and baked goods directly from the oven offers a food-shopping experience distinctly different from that of a suburban market.

For a visitor, it's easy to fantasize about life on the farm, but the reality of that life is long days of physical labor, which probably wouldn't appeal to people accustomed to the comforts of modern life.

Walking behind a team of horses all day is a life different from working at a desk, but the bigger difference between Amish life and life for most other Americans is philosophical. The Amish don't consider the acquisition of material wealth a worthy goal, and that's an idea that is foreign to most Americans.

The reality is that nobody joins the Amish. They're basically a closed society that grows not by recruiting new members but by having children. So it's intriguing and safe to look at them from the comfort of an air-conditioned car and to imagine leading their style of life. (If you want to get a true taste of farm life, try a farm vacation. Some farmers take in guests and let them see what the farm life really is. See "Lodging.")

Visitors don't make the conversion to the Amish religion, but the 1980s movie *Witness* portrayed a romance between an Amish woman and a non-Amish man. That's possible, but highly unlikely, and it's hard to imagine a sophisticated city guy marrying into an Amish family and moving to the farm.

So it's unlikely that any visitors will ever become Amish, but observing the Amish lifestyle is the attraction that draws visitors to Lancaster County and brings them back again and again.

The land itself is also an attraction. In summer, all is green, as the narrow country roads become mere asphalt ribbons through canyons of corn. The roads are winding and discourage fast driving, and on many roads, buggies and bicycles outnumber cars. In a seventy-miles-per-hour world, Lancaster County offers a pleasant twelve-miles-per-hour alternative.

Beyond the Amish

The Amish are Lancaster County's best-known and most visible attraction, but they're just one of many reasons why visitors flock to the area. Even without the Amish, Lancaster County has much to offer. It's a historically important region that has much to interest visitors, and in the past decade or so, Lancaster County has developed two new identities (theatre and shopping) that literally bring in visitors by the busload. In addition, Lancaster County has three excellent attractions (covered bridges, recreational bicycling, and outdoor recreation) that receive little publicity and thus attract few visitors. Add in railroads, antiques, and food, and you'll find plenty of reasons to enjoy a weekend or a week in Amish Country, even if you don't go looking for the Amish.

So whatever your pleasure may be, you're almost certain to find it in Lancaster County. (Well, the ocean isn't here.) So come and enjoy, but please be courteous. And remember, the Amish are real people leading real lives.

Visitor's Etiquette

The Amish would prefer not to be the objects of tourists' attention, but they've grown accustomed to it. Still, it's important to keep in mind that they're not actors, that their farms and businesses are workplaces, and that their homes are private.

Around Lancaster County, everyone has heard stories of tourists walking into an Amish home or becoming upset when the Amish wouldn't pose for pictures. Such incidents show a lack of understanding of who the Amish are and a lack of courtesy. Such an incident might also result in an injury, because farms, like many workplaces, can be dangerous. Farms don't have Employees Only signs, as some other businesses do, so visitors should always stay away from the working parts of a farm or a business on a farm.

Amish is a religion, and in that sense, the Amish are no different from Orthodox Jews, Hindus, or members of any other religious group who wear clothes that identify them with their religion. Few people would drive through a Jewish or Hindu neighborhood gawking and snapping pictures, but it happens all the time to the Amish.

Still, it's possible to be a polite visitor. Just treat everyone with respect and remember that the Amish frown on photographs that involve them.

Information Sources

Pennsylvania Dutch Convention and Visitors Bureau
501 Greenfield Road Lancaster (Greenfield Road exit of Route 30)
www.padutchcountry.com
This is the primary visitor's center in Lancaster County.

Amish Mennonite Information Center
Route 340, Old Philadelphia Pike, Intercourse
(717) 768-0807

Downtown Visitors Information Center
100 S. Queen Street, Lancaster
(717) 397-3531

Lititz Welcome Center
18 N. Broad Street (Route 501) (beside railroad tracks in restored
   train station)
(717) 626-8981

Mennonite Information Center
2209 Millstream Road, Lancaster (beside Tanger Outlets on
   Route 30 East)
(717) 299-0954, www.mennoniteinfoctr.com

Susquehanna Heritage Tourist and Information Center
5th and Linden streets, Columbia (at Route 441 exit of Route 30)
(717) 684-5249

Quick Facts

Emergencies—Dial 911

Time zone—Eastern

Alcoholic beverages—The legal age is 21. Bringing alcohol from other states is illegal. Taverns and distributors sell beer. Liquor is available only through state stores and by the drink in taverns and some restaurants.

Driving—Minimum age for drivers is 16.

Legal holidays— January 1, Martin Luther King's birthday (third Monday in January), Presidents' Day (third Monday in February), Memorial Day, July 4, Labor Day, Columbus Day (second Monday in October), Veterans Day (November 11), Thanksgiving, and Christmas

Note: Amish people do not celebrate secular holidays, only Christian ones.

Local Television Stations—Channel 8—WGAL, NBC; Channel 15—WLYH, UPN; Channel 21—WHP, CBS; Channel 27—WHTM, ABC; Channel 33—WITF, PBS; Channel 43—WPMT, FOX

Getting There

Lancaster County is close to most of the major cities on the East Coast. It's 70 miles to Philadelphia and Baltimore, 110 to

Washington, and 160 to New York. The Pennsylvania Turnpike has two interchanges in Lancaster County and one a mile away. U.S. Route 30 is a busy road that runs through the county and provides easy access to Baltimore and Washington through its intersection with I-83 in York.

Amtrak serves Lancaster, and the county has an airport. Harrisburg International Airport, a much larger facility, is in Middletown, between Lancaster and Harrisburg.

Weather

Lancaster County has four distinct seasons, and the trend through the late 1990s and the years 2000-2002 was toward mild winters. The winter of 2001-2002 only brought 10 inches of snow, but the average is much more than that.

Winters can be very cold, and summers can be very hot. Basically, it's the same climate as there is in every other place at 40 degrees north latitude. Anything meteorological can happen, but overall, Lancaster's weather is pretty mild.

Colorful Names

How far is it from Intercourse to Paradise? In Lancaster County, it's about 3 miles, and the route will take you through a covered bridge.

Lancaster County has a collection of colorful names, such as

- Intercourse
- Paradise
- Blue Ball
- Bird-in-Hand
- White Horse
- Black Barren
- Fertility
- Pequea (not a colorful name but one whose pronunciation no one ever guesses correctly—it's *Peck' way.*

GUIDE TO THE
Amish
Country

Who Are the Amish?

Amish is a Christian religion that's also a complete lifestyle. Some people wind themselves up for an hour of religion every Sunday, but the Amish base their entire lives around their religion. It defines how they dress, travel, and work. The Amish are Anabaptists, meaning that they believe in adult baptism. Because of that belief, many young people own cars and boats on Amish property. Until they choose to join the church, usually when they prepare to marry, young people aren't officially Amish. That allows them to own cars and boats and anything else that they choose.

The Amish religion actually encourages young people to experience the outside world for awhile. The theory is that they'll choose the Amish life over the "English" life, and the statistics support the theory. Most people born into the Amish faith choose to join the church, and those who do leave find that the glitter of the outside world isn't necessarily better than the closely bound community in which they grew up. Subsequently, many return to the faith.

Thus, schoolchildren aren't officially Amish, neither are many teenagers, and if you can recognize their dress, you may see them filling up their cars and trucks at gas stations along Route 340 on a Sunday afternoon. That may not conform to outsiders' ideas of what the Amish should be, but they're really not concerned with others' opinions.

Wash day, Amish farm

Amish school, Stumptown Road

What matter most to the Amish are God, family, and work. Their choice not to embrace much that is modern doesn't come from a belief that modern things are inherently evil. Instead, it comes from a judgment of what's best for their families and for their community as a whole.

For example, the Amish don't believe that cars, buses, and bicycles are bad things. Instead, they've made the judgment that a man who owns a car might spend his nights away from home instead of with his family, so they choose not to use cars—which doesn't mean that they never travel by motor vehicle.

The Amish of Lancaster County often travel to a community near Sarasota, Florida, and they use motor vehicles to get there. Some Amish farm down there, and many others vacation there. During the winter months, a bus company in Lancaster County makes regular runs to Florida. Around Lancaster County, some people make a living transporting the Amish over distances that are too much for a buggy, so it's inaccurate to say that the Amish never use cars and buses.

They also use electricity, but they won't buy it from public utility companies. Instead, they produce their own from various sources. And they're not immune from government regulations. They pay taxes and they must keep the milk they produce refrigerated until a truck picks it up.

A list of written or oral rules, known as Ordnung, defines all aspects of Amish life. The rules in Ordnung explain the basics of the faith and help to define what it means to be Amish. For an Amish person, the Ordnung describes almost every part of life, from dress and hair length to buggy style and farming techniques. The Ordnung will vary from community to community and order to order, which explains why you will see some Amish using electricity and riding in automobiles, while others don't even accept the use of battery-powered lights.

Lancaster's Amish are relatively progressive. Other Amish groups, such as the Nebraska Amish (who have a settlement near State College in central Pennsylvania), almost totally reject modern technology.

Cows

WATER
TO
COOL
YOUR
HORSE
→

A sign you won't see everywhere

Amish Education

Amish children receive eight years of schooling, all in the same one-room school, which is generally very close to home. Throughout Lancaster County there are more than one hundred fifty one-room schools, about $^2/_3$ Amish and $^1/_3$ Mennonite. The schools teach basic skills but not religion. That's a job for the parents. The fathers take care of the school buildings, and it's not unusual to see sheep mowing the grass at an Amish school.

Despite the relatively short duration of their schooling, the Amish learn the basics of reading, writing, and arithmetic very well, and many are excellent business owners. From early childhood, they learn lessons of responsibility, hard work, and efficiency at home. These are lessons that come in handy when running a farm and a business.

The history of Amish parochial schools is actually rather short, and it wasn't a religious issue that led them to establish their own schools. Until the late 1930s, Amish children went to public schools. Then, the issues of consolidation and busing inspired the Amish to develop their own school system.

When public schools were small and local, parents felt that they had a measure of control over what went on inside, so the idea of sending their children many miles away to go to school just didn't work for the Amish. They feared losing control of what their children would learn, and busing had a very practical drawback. Time spent on a bus was time not spent working on the farm.

After many years of debate with government officials, the Supreme Court, in 1972, decided that the Amish had the right to educate their children as they chose, and the Amish school system has been growing ever since, as has the Mennonite school system.

How can you tell the difference between the schools of the Amish and the Mennonites? Here's a *wheel* good clue. At Amish schools, you'll see scooters. At Mennonite schools, you'll see bicycles. Generally, the Amish don't use bicycles, but

Mennonite school, Terre Hill

for Mennonites, they're an important mode of transportation. If you see a school with both bicycles and scooters on the campus, it's a school with both Amish and Mennonite students.

Where Are the Amish?

Overall, the Amish are in twenty states in America and in Canada, with the largest populations being in Pennsylvania, Ohio, and Indiana. Holmes County, Ohio, has the largest Amish population, about eighteen thousand, a number slightly larger than that of Lancaster County.

Lancaster County's Amish population would be larger if more farms were available, but the county is full, and some Amish families from Lancaster County have moved to neighboring counties and out of the area. Lebanon, York, Chester, and Berks counties all border Lancaster County and all have Amish populations.

Within Lancaster County, the eastern part of the county—around the towns of New Holland, Bird-in-Hand, Intercourse, Paradise, and Strasburg—has been and still is the traditional Amish stronghold. Not coincidentally, that's the region that is home to the vast majority of Lancaster County's tourist attractions. All of the businesses and tourist attractions with *Amish* in their names are in the eastern part of the county, along routes 340, 30, 741, and 896.

The Amish stronghold is in the eastern parts, but the Amish are moving to other parts of the county as well. They now have districts around Manheim in the northwest and Quarryville in the south. They go where the farms are, and in Lancaster County, farms are everywhere. Many residents of Lancaster would like to see the Amish buy up every farm in the county, so that the developers couldn't turn them into houses and shopping centers.

The Amish and Money

The Amish are frugal, not poor. In their culture, the acquisition of wealth simply for the sake of having impressive material goods is unacceptable. But that doesn't mean that they

Donkeys

don't have any money. In fact, their farms have much value just for the land, and they run some very successful nonfarm businesses. When they do make money, their preferred use is to buy more farms for their children.

The Amish and Work

For many people, work is a means to an end. Work is the

means to pay the bills and have fun. To the Amish, work is something different. It's a way to make money to pay the bills, but it also has its own inherent worth. The Amish work because their faith tells them that work has value. Besides, they don't have televisions to sit in front of all day.

Where the Mennonites Are

Mennonites are another Anabaptist sect, and they have the same religious roots as the Amish. In fact, the Amish broke off from the Mennonites in Europe back in the seventeenth century. Today, Mennonites are much more numerous than the Amish, and Mennonites come in many degrees of worldliness. They live in cities and have high schools and universities. They also have Old Order Mennonites who drive buggies and Black Bumper Mennonites who drive cars—but only cars that are black all over, including the bumpers.

Mennonites live everywhere, from New York City to missions in Africa to farms in rural Lancaster County. The Amish and Mennonites have differences in dress and in the styles of their buggies, but to someone who has never seen either group before, they do look very similar.

Some Mennonite children go to school for only eight years, arriving by buggy, but other Mennonite students drive cars to Lancaster Mennonite High School, and its athletic teams compete with local public schools in many sports. From there, students move on to Eastern Mennonite University and other Mennonite colleges and universities, as well as to secular institutions.

Tourists have followed the Amish closely but have paid little attention to the Mennonites. Lancaster County has a Mennonite Information Center and more Mennonites than Amish, but the title of this book doesn't contain the word *Mennonite*.

What that means is that if you want to get a look at the real Lancaster County, specifically the rural places where the tourists rarely venture, you'll do just as well to travel through

Mennonite areas and Amish areas. To the untrained eye, a Mennonite buggy looks like an Amish buggy, but in Mennonite areas, tourists are far fewer in numbers.

The highest concentration of Mennonites is in the northeastern part of Lancaster County, in places such as Martindale, Terre Hill, and Farmersville. On those roads, you'll see many bicycles, and in 2002, a Mennonite resident of Farmersville rode his bike much faster than the Mennonite girls in pastel dresses ever ride over those country roads. Floyd Landis, a graduate of Conestoga Valley High School in Lancaster, completed the Tour de France as a teammate of Lance Armstrong. Local papers carried the story that his mother had to go to a friend's home to watch her son on television because her family has never had a television in the home. Another story said that Floyd Landis had to ask permission from his pastor to wear the flashy spandex uniforms that cyclists favor.

On the roads around Farmersville, bikes and buggies are just about as common as cars, and on Sunday mornings, the roads are full of bikes, buggies, and black-bumper cars, all heading to church. It's a sight that you won't see on the streets of New York or Philadelphia.

A6mish and Mennonite History

In 1536, Menno Simons, a Catholic priest from Holland, joined the Anabaptist movement. He had the ability to unite many of the Anabaptist groups, and they subsequently acquired the nickname Mennonites.

In 1693, Jakob Ammann, a Swiss bishop, broke away from the main group of Mennonites, and his followers became the Amish. The groups have differences in beliefs, and they have split several times, but the Amish and Mennonite churches still share the same beliefs concerning adult baptism and many aspects of faith.

As part of William Penn's "holy experiment" of religious tolerance and freedom, the Amish and Mennonites both settled in Pennsylvania. The first sizable group of Amish arrived in Lancaster County in the 1720s or 1730s.

Sign

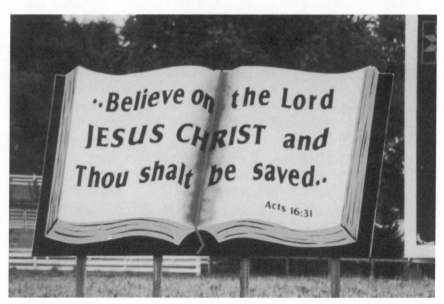

Sign

While both groups' beliefs have many similarities, they're distinctly different in some ways. For example, the Mennonites have churches, while the Amish conduct their worship services in congregation at members' homes on a rotating basis. Together, they make up a rather small percentage of Lancaster County's residents, but they own a large percentage of the land, and their buggies are an image closely associated with Lancaster County.

Lancaster County also has a third group of Anabaptists: the Brethren. They get little publicity, but they're an important part of the Lancaster community.

Pennsylvania Dutch Stuff

The term *Pennsylvania Dutch* is common in Lancaster and the surrounding counties. It describes both a people and a culture, but it has nothing to do with Holland.

In this instance, *Dutch* is an altered spelling of *Deutsche*—German. Many of the residents of south-central Pennsylvania can trace their roots to Germany and countries where German is a common language, and *Pennsylvania Dutch* refers to these people.

The Amish are a part of the Pennsylvania Dutch, but not all Pennsylvania Dutch people are Amish. They come in many religions, and they live in many counties. They even have their own Pennsylvania Dutch language and a distinctive accent. Across the region you'll see the word *Dutch* in the names of many sorts of businesses, from Dutch Wonderland Amusement Park to Dutch Apple Dinner Theatre.

You may even hear a slogan describing the Pennsylvania Dutch heritage: "If you ain't Dutch, you ain't much." If you do hear it, though, take it with a chuckle. Pennsylvania Dutch people are, as a group, hardworking, humble, and helpful.

Lancaster County
Yesterday and Today

By American standards, Lancaster County has a long history. Historical records indicate the establishment of a residence in Nobleville in eastern Lancaster County in 1691. By the early 1700s, settlers were trickling in, and Lancaster County's oldest remaining building, the Hans Herr House in Willow Street, dates to 1719. Seeking religious freedom, Amish settlers arrived by 1730, but since everyone rode in buggies then, no one noticed.

Geography, natural resources, and ingenuity have made Lancaster County a major player in American history. The Conestoga wagon, the vehicle that transported hundreds of thousands of settlers across the country, is a Lancaster County invention.

During the Revolutionary War, Lancaster was a major producer of guns and ammunition and a major food supplier for American troops. Despite its name, the Kentucky rifle is actually a Pennsylvania product.

For a day during the Revolutionary War, Lancaster was the capital of the new nation. That happened because members of the government stopped here on their way to York, which served as capital for half a year.

In 1794, the nation's first turnpike opened, linking Philadelphia and Lancaster. That road helped to establish

Conestoga wagon, Kitchen Kettle Village, Intercourse

Lancaster County as a major supplier of agricultural products for the rest of the nation.

Lancaster was a busy stop on the main line of the Pennsylvania Railroad, and when Horseshoe Curve opened at Altoona in 1854, it immediately became a tourist attraction and brought many people through Lancaster.

As the nation expanded, Lancaster grew in size and wealth. The architecture of the city of Lancaster speaks of a prosperous place, and a walk within half a mile of Penn Square will lead to many elegant homes built in the nineteenth century.

In the 1860s, the company that is now Armstrong World Industries purchased a piece of property beside the railroad tracks for a new plant, and today this company is still Lancaster's biggest manufacturer.

The farm economy is more visible than manufacturing, but Lancaster has always had a strong manufacturing economy, and today many Amish families have small manufacturing operations on their farms.

For many reasons, Lancaster has prospered. The economy has always been diverse—with strength in agriculture, manufacturing, and tourism—and the work ethic is strong. Consequently, that economic strength, coupled with the beauty of the place, has created growth problems.

Suburban sprawl is as much of a concern in Lancaster as it is anywhere else. Houses rise daily from fields that grew corn a year earlier, and builders have learned to expect opposition whenever they propose new developments. In response to the sprawl, the county as a whole has become very sensitive to growth issues. No one expects to stop growth, but many groups are working hard to funnel building projects into already developed areas, and the county has established urban growth boundaries in an attempt to keep new construction in already developed areas.

Growth is occurring, but it doesn't mean that every rural road ends at a shopping center. The areas affected by sprawl are the most visible ones because they're closest to the highways, but rural Lancaster County is still strong, and statistics show that the vast majority of the land in Lancaster County does not grow suburban houses or shopping centers. More than $2/3$ of the land is still farmland, and about 15 percent of the land is woodland, which means that about $5/6$ of the land area is growing either crops or trees.

For a visitor, that means that it is possible to ride a bike down country roads where one Amish farm runs into another and where buggies outnumber cars. Lancaster County is by far Pennsylvania's most productive agricultural county, and it's still possible to find places where barefoot children walk from their farm homes to one-room schools, maybe even going through a covered bridge on the way.

Everything modern has come to Lancaster County, but the old traditions are still strong. Away from the busy highways, Lancaster County is still a quiet, rural place.

Highways and Back Roads

Lancaster County covers 946 square miles, which is about 90 percent of Rhode Island's land area. The vast majority of the Amish-related tourist businesses lie in a relatively small area bounded by Route 340 on the north, Route 741 on the south, the city of Lancaster on the west, and Route 41 on the east.

Route 30 East is pure tourism. Take away the references to the Amish on a few of the businesses and Route 30 could be Anywhere, U.S.A.

Route 340 lies several miles north of and parallel to Route 30. Route 340 gets crowded at times, but it's significantly different from Route 340. If Route 30 represents big business, Route 340 represents family businesses. (One interesting way to see the difference is to visit on a Sunday. All of the businesses on Route 30 are open, while many of the businesses on Route 340 are closed for the Sabbath.)

Route 896, from Route 340 south to the town of Strasburg, is home to many tourist businesses, including Sight and Sound Theatre, Lancaster County's newest big attraction.

Route 741 in Strasburg becomes crowded at times, but the attractions are all close together. The road covers many miles in Lancaster County, but the only tourist attractions are on its two-mile Strasburg stretch.

Route 30

Route 30 East—Anywhere, U.S.A.

Route 30 East still goes by the name Lincoln Highway. It was the country's first transcontinental highway, but in Lancaster County, you'll find almost nothing to remind you of that era. Farther west, the Lincoln Highway Association remembers earlier eras in the life of the automobile, but in the eastern half of Lancaster County, Route 30 is a busy, wide highway, filled with cars and trucks.

In many ways, it's indistinguishable from similar stretches of highway all across the country. It is home to familiar restaurants and motels, and if you prefer to eat and sleep in places that you recognize, Route 30 will be your comfort zone.

That doesn't mean that Route 30 doesn't have any attractions unique to Lancaster County, but it's definitely the busiest stretch of highway in the region.

If you enter Lancaster County on Route 30, be assured that the entire county isn't so crowded. In fact, in the eastern half of the county, Route 30 is a wave of chaos in a sea of tranquility. Turn off Route 30 on Belmont Road in Paradise and in half a mile you'll pass through a covered bridge frequented by Amish buggies.

From Paradise west to Route 462, Route 30 is home to tourist businesses, restaurants, and motels. Shopping centers are also common, and trucks and tour buses fill the highway. Route 30 is not the place to get the feeling of a quaint country town, but it does have plenty of places to visit, eat, and sleep.

Route 340—America's First Turnpike

Route 340, the Old Philadelphia Pike, was part of the nation's first turnpike. Opening in 1794, the Lancaster Turnpike linked Philadelphia and Lancaster and promoted commerce between the two cities. The original turnpike was 68 miles, and in a few places, marker stones still sit beside the highway with numbers such as L-6 and P-62, meaning six miles to Lancaster and 62 to Philadelphia.

Today, Route 340 has two distinctly different characters in Lancaster County. From the Chester County line west to the village of Intercourse, it's a country road that carries relatively light traffic. It's a two-lane highway and not as conducive to truck traffic as Route 30 is.

From Intercourse west to Lancaster, Route 340 is both a busy local road and a busy tourist road. In Intercourse and Bird-in-Hand are concentrations of tourist businesses, and Amish buggies are common sights on the road.

On Sundays, an interesting difference between routes 30 and 340 is visible. Basically, Route 30 is open while Route 340 is closed. Most of the businesses on Route 340 are family businesses, and they close to observe the Sabbath. In contrast, businesses on Route 30 are open. So a Sunday drive down Route 340 will be scenic, but you won't be able to visit many of the attractions. A few are open, but if you're planning to visit any

place on Route 340, avoid disappointment and call ahead to
see if it's open on Sunday.

The Connector—Route 896

Route 896 is the major north-south route through the heart
of the tourist region. Beginning at Route 340, it extends southeast to the Chester County line. From Route 340 south to
Strasburg, it's a busy local and tourist road with many Amish
buggies on it. Southeast of Strasburg, it's a country road with
few businesses and no tourist attractions.

The Iron Road—Route 741

Half a dozen railroad attractions make Route 741 in
Strasburg Lancaster County's version of the Iron Road. The
attractions cluster around the eastern side of Strasburg.
Otherwise, Route 741 is a wide-open road that runs through
the heart of Amish farm country. In downtown Strasburg, the
road can become very busy during prime season.

Here's a look at some other highways that pass through
Lancaster County.

PA 23 begins in Marietta, near the Susquehanna River, and
crosses the county from west to east. Just beyond the Lancaster
County border, it intersects the Pennsylvania Turnpike at
Morgantown.

On the western edge of Lancaster, where Route 23 is
Marietta Avenue, lies Wheatland, home of Pres. James
Buchanan. The route has sections where it's rural, suburban,
and urban. In the eastern part of Lancaster County, it serves as
Main Street in Leola, New Holland, Blue Ball, Goodville, and
Churchtown. It's a busy local road with few tourist attractions.

PA 41 extends from Route 30 at Gap to the Chester County
line, and it's a good road to avoid—full of trucks and not very
enjoyable.

PA 72 runs from the northern edge of Lancaster through East

Wheatland, home of Pres. James Buchanan, Lancaster

Susquehanna River at Marietta

Petersburg, Manheim, and Mount Gretna, where it has an interchange with the Pennsylvania Turnpike (Lancaster/Lebanon). An interesting place to visit is Cloister Car Wash, about a mile and a half north of Lancaster. It holds the distinction of being the world's largest car wash. For most of its length, Route 72 is a busy highway.

U.S. Route 222 runs the entire length of the county from north to south. The northern portion of the road is a four-lane, divided highway. From Lancaster to the Maryland state line, it's two lanes. South of Willow Street, it's a busy rural road that passes through the town of Quarryville. Along the highway, south of Quarryville, is the birthplace of Robert Fulton, inventor of the steamboat.

PA 272 parallels U.S. Route 222 through much of the county. In the northern part of the county, PA 272 was PA 222 before the building of the divided highway. This highway has a number of interesting attractions from the Pennsylvania

Green Dragon Market, Ephrata

Streetlight in Hershey

Turnpike south to the city of Lancaster, including the antiques shops of Adamstown, the Ephrata Cloister, and the Green Dragon Market and Auction.

PA 283 is a four-lane, divided highway that extends from the western side of Lancaster to Harrisburg. It blends with U.S. 30 just west of Lancaster and intersects the Pennsylvania Turnpike near Steelton in Dauphin County.

U.S. 322 runs diagonally from Blue Ball to Ephrata to Hershey. It's a busy road through Mennonite farm country around Blue Ball and Hinkletown, and it's home to many roadside produce stands. It also passes the Ephrata Cloister, then goes near Cornwall Iron Furnace and Mount Gretna before reaching Hershey.

PA 324 runs from Lancaster to the Susquehanna River at Pequea.

PA 501 runs from Lancaster to Lancaster County, passing through Lititz in northern Lancaster County. Along much of its route, it's a busy suburban road.

PA 772 runs from Route 30, near Gap, to Marietta, taking a circuitous route through Intercourse, Leola, Lititz, Manheim, and Mount Joy.

Lancaster Towns and Neighbors

Adamstown bills itself as Antiques Capital, U.S.A., and has actually trademarked the name. Adamstown lies at Exit 21 of the Pennsylvania Turnpike, and that easy access has made it a favorite meeting place for buyers and sellers of antiques. The biggest names are Renninger's and Shupp's Grove, and they and many other dealers combine to form a mile of antiques shops along Route 272. Many shops are open only on weekends, and on Saturdays and Sundays, the traffic is heavy throughout the region.

Adamstown's other big attraction is Stoudtburg, a re-creation of a German town that features tall houses with businesses on the ground floor, a brewery, a beer garden, and an antiques mall.

For information on Adamstown, check www.antiquescapital. com.

Bird-in-Hand is a village along Route 340 in the heart of Amish Country. The biggest attraction in town is the Bird-in-Hand Farmers' Market, but many other attractions bring in visitors. The region is relatively flat, and it's a favorite with bicyclists.

The name of the village comes from a time when most people couldn't read. The owner of an inn created a sign that showed a man with a bird in his hand to serve as an identifying mark for travelers, and the name stuck. Today, visitors come to Bird-in-Hand for a look at Amish life and for shopping opportunities.

Churchtown is a scenic hamlet on Route 23 in the eastern part of the county. Named for its many churches, it offers broad views

Renninger's Antique Market, Adamstown

of the Conestoga Valley. Churchtown doesn't have much in the way of attractions, but it does have a nice collection of inns and bed and breakfasts. An interesting place to visit is Smucker's Harness Shop. Located on an Amish farm, the shop makes and sells harnesses for all types of horses, from farm horses to horse-show horses. The shop also carries everything needed to keep a horse healthy and happy.

Columbia is the biggest river town in Lancaster County. Located on the wide Susquehanna, it's an industrial town trying to build attraction for tourists, and it has some interesting places to visit.

At the top of the list (literally) is Chickies Rock County Park, which looms high above the river along Route 441 and provides hiking trails and great views. In town is the National Watch and Clock Museum, which provides a fascinating look at timepieces throughout the ages.

If you look into the river, you can see the supports for the longest covered bridge ever built. The last bridge on the site washed away in 1896, but the supports are still there.

Ephrata is home to the Ephrata Cloister, an early and success-ful effort in communal living. Ephrata's biggest attraction is the Green Dragon Market and Auction, a vast flea market that oper-ates only on Fridays. Another attraction is Ten Thousand Villages, a shopping and eating complex operated by the Mennonite Church. It features crafts and foods from many parts of the world, with a menu from a different country each week.

Intercourse is a village on Route 340 in the eastern part of the county. It's a favorite with visitors, with a heavy concentration of attractions in a small space. Kitchen Kettle Village is a collection of shops and restaurants.

Lititz, for a century after its founding in 1756 by the Moravian Church, was a closed community. Today, the Moravian influence is still visible, but the town is a diverse place where visitors enjoy walking along tree-lined streets and shopping in small stores. Right in the center of town is Sturgis Pretzel Bakery, America's oldest, dating to 1861. Lititz Springs Park, along Route 501 at the

Amish buggy in Intercourse

National Watch and Clock Museum, Columbia

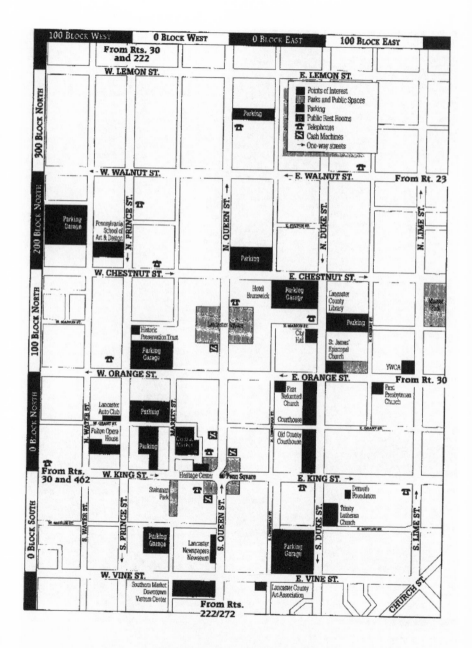

Downtown Lancaster

railroad tracks, is the site of many community events, including a large craft show in July. For much more information, visit www.LititzPa.com.

Mount Joy is a pleasant little town far from the areas of heavy tourist traffic. One attraction that does draw visitors is Bube's Brewery, an intact nineteenth-century brewery that now houses a bar and several restaurants, including the Catacombs, which is 43 feet below ground. On Sunday evenings in summer, Music in the Park in Memorial Park offers a bit of small-town Americana.

New Holland is a town of heavy industries surrounded by Amish farmlands in eastern Lancaster County. It's close to the heavily traveled tourist areas, but it really isn't an active tourist destination. It is, however, a heavy manufacturing area, and the New Holland brand of farm equipment and industrial machinery, made here, is known around the world.

One attraction in New Holland is the New Holland Band, a community band that began in 1829. The band plays all over Lancaster and the surrounding counties, and its home field is New Holland Community Park. It also performs at the New Holland Fair, which turns the streets of New Holland into a community celebration during the first week of October. For the band's schedule, visit www.newhollandband.org.

Strasburg is Traintown, U.S.A. The Strasburg RailRoad, Railroad Museum of Pennsylvania, Toy Train Museum, Red Caboose Motel, and a variety of train shops make this a rail fan's delight. Also in Strasburg is Sight and Sound Millennium Theatre, which produces Biblical stage shows. The Strasburg Creamery, on the square, is an old-fashioned ice-cream and soda shop.

Terre Hill (The Town That Time Ignored). If you're looking for a true getaway in Lancaster County, head for the little town of Terre Hill. Few tourists ever wander there, and many Lancastrians don't even know where it is. That combination makes it a great place to visit if you're the type who can enjoy a truly leisurely getaway.

Other than a park with a great view of the Conestoga Valley, Terre Hill has no tourist attractions but is a beautiful place.

Sight and Sound Millennium Theatre, Strasburg
"And the wolf shall dwell with the lamb." —Isa. 11:6

Perched on a little hill in the northeastern part (the borders are too irregular to call it a corner) of Lancaster County, Terre Hill has a restaurant, convenience store, park with a hidden covered bridge, a chiropractor, and one bed and breakfast. That's about it, except for one weekend in July when the celebration of Terre Hill Days turns the town from mild to wild as the place becomes one big yard sale.

In Terre Hill, you can walk from one end of town to the other—in about 10 minutes. You can sit in the park and enjoy the view. You can watch the buggies roll by. (*Hint:* These are Mennonite, not Amish). You can also ride your bike on the lightly traveled roads in the region.

If you're looking for action, you won't find it in this town, but it's not far away, either. A few miles north on Route 897 is Weaver's Store, known by some as the Mennonite Mall. Weaver's is a general store with a little bit of a lot of things, and it's always busy. The store probably doesn't carry any items that you can't find elsewhere, but the prices are pretty good.

If you continue north and turn on School Road, then on Crest View Drive, you'll come to Hawk Valley Golf Club, an 18-hole course.

And that's about it for the attractions in and around Terre Hill.

Nice Neighbors

Lancaster County offers a wide variety of attractions, and because county lines are meaningless to visitors, the surrounding region offers much more. Consider that from downtown Lancaster, it's only about

25 miles to **York**
25 miles to **Hershey**
35 miles to **Reading**
50 miles to **Gettysburg**

The wide Susquehanna River separates Lancaster and York counties, but they have a shared history, and they've begun a joint program called Heritage Tourism to celebrate that history.

York has a huge industrial history, and it has recently developed its own niche in the tourist world as the Factory-Tour Capital of the World. Visitors to factories making everything from potato chips to motorcycles can see how raw materials become finished products. By far the most famous plant in York is **Harley Davidson Motorcycles.**

Another very popular attraction in York is the **York County Heritage Rail Trail.** The trail begins in downtown York and extends about 22 miles in Pennsylvania and 24 more in Maryland. It's tremendously popular with runners, bikers, and walkers. For information on York, consult the **York County Convention and Visitors Bureau,** 155 West Market Street, York, (717) 852-9675 or (888) 858-YORK, www.yorkpa.org.

Twenty-five miles west of York (and 50 miles west of Lancaster) is **Gettysburg,** where the Civil War is still the biggest business. Millions of visitors pour in every year to see the site of America's bloodiest battle. **Gettysburg Convention and Visitors Bureau**, 35 Carlisle Street, Gettysburg, (717) 334-6274, www.gettysburg.com.

Reading is 35 miles northeast of Lancaster, and outlet shopping began there. It's still big business. Reading is also home to the Reading Phillies AA baseball team, Reading Royals minorleague hockey team, and the Daniel Boone Homestead. **Reading and Berks County Visitors Bureau**, 352 Penn Street, Reading, (610) 375-4085 or (800) 443-6610, www.readingberkspa.com.

Hershey is 25 miles from Lancaster, and it's Chocolatetown, U.S.A., the sweetest place on earth. It's home to Hershey Foods, which makes Hershey Chocolate. The biggest attraction is HersheyPark, home to many roller coasters and other exciting rides. 100 West Hersheypark Drive, (800) HERSHEY, www.hersheypa.com.

Lodging

Lancaster County has plenty of rooms and plenty of variety, but that doesn't mean that you can always drop in unexpectedly and find the exact accommodations you want. The place gets busy, especially at predictable times, and sometimes at unlikely times, such as Presidents' Day weekend in February. If the weather's nice, people come to cure cabin fever. Plus, Presidents' Day weekend is close to Valentine's Day, and Hershey, the sweetest place on earth, is just 25 miles away.

Summer is consistently busy, but October is actually the busiest month for tourism in Lancaster County. If you really want to escape the crowds, come in December or January. They're pretty slow months.

Regardless of when you come, it's wise to call ahead for reservations.

Lancaster County Reservation Center, (800) 723-8824, www.padutchlodging.com

Motels

1722 Motor Lodge, 1722 Old Philadelphia Pike (Route 340), **Lancaster,** (717) 397-4791

Akron Motel, 116 S. Seventh Street (Route 272), **Akron,** (717) 859-1654 or (877) 274-6009, www.motelakron.com

The Amish Country

BIRD IN HAND PA

MOTEL

NO VACANCY

Reservations suggested

Amish Country Motel, 3013 Old Philadelphia Pike (Route 340), **Bird-in-Hand**, (717) 768-8396 or (800) 538-2535, www.bird-in-hand.com/amishcountry

Amish Lanterns Motel, Hartman Bridge Road (Route 896), **Strasburg**, (717) 687-7839

Beaver Creek Farm Cabins, 2 Little Beaver Road, **Strasburg**, (717) 687-7745, www.beavercreekfarmcabins.com

Bird-in-Hand Family Inn, 2740 Old Philadelphia Pike (Route 340), **Bird-in-Hand**, (717) 768-8271 or (800) 537-2535, www.bird-in-hand.com/familyinn

Black Horse Lodge and Suites, 2180 North Reading Road (Route 272), **Denver**, (717) 336-7563 or (800) 610-3805, www.blackhorselodge.com

Canadiana Motor Inn, 2390 Lincoln Highway East (Route 30), **Lancaster**, (717) 397-6531 or (888) 397-6531

Carriage House Motor Inn, 144 East Main Street (Route 741), **Strasburg**, (717) 687-7651, www.amishcountryinns.com

Classic Inn, 2302 Lincoln Highway East (Route 30), **Lancaster**, (717) 291-4576 or (888) 395-3262

Comfort Inn New Holland, 626 West Main Street (Route 23), **New Holland**, (717) 355-9900 or (800) 296-4661, www.comfortinnnewholland.com

Comfort Inn Sherwood Knoll, 500 Centerville Road, **Lancaster**, (717) 898-2431 or (800) 223-8963, www.comfortlancaster.com

Continental Inn, 2285 Lincoln Highway East (Route 30), **Lancaster**, (717) 299-0421, www.continentalinn.com

Country Inn and Suites, **Lancaster**, 2260 Lincoln Highway East (Route 30), **Lancaster**, (717) 299-4460 or (800) 456-4000, www.countryinns.com/lancasterpa

Country Inn and Suites by Carlson, 1475 Lancaster Road (Route 72), **Manheim**, (717) 665-5440 or (800) 456-4000, www.countryinns.com

Country Inn of Lancaster, 2133 Lincoln Highway East (Route 30), **Lancaster**, (717) 393-3413 or (877) 393-3413, www.countryinnoflancaster.com

Country Living Inn, 2406 Old Philadelphia Pike (Route 340), **Lancaster**, (717) 295-7295, www.countrylivinginn.com

Countryside Motel, 134 Hartman Bridge Road (Route 896), **Ronks**, (717) 687-8431

Days Inn East (Lancaster), 34 Route 896 North, **Ronks**, (717) 390-1800 or (800) DAYS INN

Dutch Treat Motel, Route 896 and Herr Road, **Strasburg**, (717) 687-7998, www.dutchtreatmotel.com

Eastbrook Inn, 21 Eastbrook Road, **Ronks**, (717) 393-2550 or (800) 777-8338

Econo Lodge North, 2165 Lincoln Highway East (Route 30), **Lancaster**, (717) 299-6900 or (800) 55-ECONO

Econo Lodge South, 2140 Lincoln Highway East (Route 30), (717) 397-1900 or (800) 55-ECONO

Fairfield Inn by Marriott, Lancaster, 150 Granite Run Drive, **Lancaster**, (717) 581-1800 or (800) 228-2800, www.fairfield- inn.com

Fulton Steamboat Inn, Routes 30 and 896, **Strasburg**, (717) 299-9999 or (800) 922-2229, www.fultonsteamboatinn.com

Hampton Inn—Lancaster, 545 Greenfield Road, **Lancaster,** (717) 299-1200 or (800) HAMPTON, www.hampton-inn.com

Harvest Drive Motel, 3770 Harvest Drive, **Intercourse**, (717) 768-7186 or (800) 233-0176, www.harvestdrive.com

Hawthorn Inn and Suites, 2045 Lincoln Highway East (Route 30), **Lancaster**, (717) 290-7100 or (800) 794-0735, www.hawthorn.com

Hershey Farm Inn, 240 Hartman Bridge Road (Route 896), **Ronks**, (717) 687-8635 or (800) 827-8635, www.hersheyfarm.com

Hilton Garden Inn Lancaster, 101 Granite Run Drive, **Lancaster**, (717) 560-0880, www.lancaster.gardeninn.com

Lancaster Host Resort, 2300 Lincoln Highway East (Route 30), **Lancaster**, (717) 299-5500 or (800) 233-0121, www.lancaster-host.com

Lancaster Motel, 2628 Lincoln Highway East (Route 30), **Ronks**, (717) 687-6241

Leola Village Inn and Suites, 38 Deborah Drive at Route 23, **Leola**, (717) 656-7002 or (877) 669-5094, www.leolavillage.com

Mill Stream Country Inn, 170 Eastbrook Road, **Smoketown**, (717) 299-0931 or (800) 355-1143, www.millstreamcountryinn.com

Motel 6, 2959 Lincoln Highway East (Route 30), **Gordonville**, (717) 687-3880 or (800) 4-MOTEL-6, www.motel6.com

Quiet Haven Motel, 2556 Siegrist Road, **Ronks**, (717) 397-6231

Ramada Inn Brunswick Hotel, Queen and Chestnut Streets, **Lancaster**, (717) 397-4800 or (800) 821-9258, www.hotel-brunswick.com

Smoketown Motor Lodge, 190 Eastbrook Road, **Smoketown**, (717) 397-6944, www.smoketownmotorlodge.com

Spruce Lane Lodge and Cottages, 2439 Old Philadelphia Pike (Route 30), **Lancaster**, (717) 393-1991 or (800) 446-4901, www.sprucelanelodge.com

Super 8 Motel, 2129 Lincoln Highway East (Route 30), **Lancaster**, (717) 393-8888 or (800) 800-8000, www.super8.com

Traveler's Rest Motel, 3701 Old Philadelphia Pike (Route 340), **Intercourse**, (717) 768-8731 or (800) 626-2021, www.bird-in-hand.com/travelersrest

Village Inn of Bird-in-Hand, 2695 Old Philadelphia Pike (Route 340), **Bird-in-Hand**, (717) 293-8369 or (800) 914-2473, www.bird-in-hand.com/villageinn

Weathervane Motor Court, 15 Eastbrook Road, **Ronks**, (717) 397-3398 or (866) 540-7700, www.weathervanemotorcourt.com

Willow Valley Resort and Conference Center, 2416 Willow Street Pike (Route 222), **Lancaster**, (717) 464-2711 or (800) 444-1714, www.willowvalley.com

Witmer's Tavern, Inn and Museum, 2014 Old Philadelphia Pike (Route 340), **Lancaster**, (717) 299-5305, www.bbchannel.com, www.800padutch.com/1725histwit

Zook's Motel, 103 East Main Street (Route 23), **Leola**, (717) 656-3313

Campgrounds

Beacon Hill Camping, 128 Beacon Hill Drive, **Intercourse**, (717) 768-8775, www.800padutch.com/beacon.html

Cocalico Creek Campgrounds, 560 Cocalico Road, **Denver**, (717) 336-2014, www.cocalicocreekcampground.com

Country Acres Campground, 20 Leven Road, **Godonville**, (717) 687-8014, www.countryacrescampground.com

Country Haven Campground, 354 Springville Road, **New Holland**, (717) 354-7926

Dutch Cousin Campsite, 446 Hill Road, **Denver**, (717) 336-6911 and (800) 992 0261, www.dutchcampsite.com

Flory's Cottages and Camping, 99 North Ronks Road, **Ronks**, (717) 687-6670, www.floryscamping.com

Hershey Conewago KOA Kampground, 1590 Hershey Road (Route 743), **Elizabethtown**, (717) 367-1179 or (800) KOA-7774, www.koa.com/where/pa/38123.htm

Mill Bridge Campresort, South Ronks Road, **Paradise**, (717) 687-8181 or (800) MIL-BRIG, www.millbridge.com

Oak Creek Campground, 400 East Maple Grove Road,

Bowmansville, (717) 445-6161 or (800) 446-8365, www.gocamping-america.com/oakcreekcg

Old Mill Stream Camping Manor, 2249 Lincoln Highway East (Route 30), **Lancaster**, (717) 299-2314, www.oldmillstreamcamping.com

Pinch Pond Family Campground and RV Park, 3075 Pinch Road, **Manheim**, (717) 665-7640 or (800) 659-7640, www.pinchpond.com

Red Run Campground, 877 Martin Church Road, **New Holland**, (717) 445-4526, www.redruncampground.com

Roamers' Retreat Campground, 5005 Lincoln Highway East (Route 30), **Kinzers**, (717) 442-4287 or (800) 525-5605, www.campingpa.com/roamers

Rustic Meadows Camping and Golf Resort, 1980 Turnpike Road **Elizabethtown**, (717) 367-7718 or (800) 578-7842, www.gocamping america.com/rusticmeadows

Sickman's Mill Campground, 671 Sand Hill Road, **Pequea**, (717) 872-5951

Spring Gulch Resort Campground, 475 Lynch Road, **New Holland**, (717) 354-3100 or (800) 255-5744

Starlite Camping Resort, 1500 Furnace Hill Road, **Stevens**, PA 17578, (717) 733-9655

Sun Valley Campground, Maple Grove Road, **Bowmansville**, (717) 445-6262 or (800) 700-3370, www.sunvalleycampground.net

Tucquan Park Family Campground, 917 River Road, **Holtwood**, (717) 284-2156, www.camptucquanpark.com

White Oak Campground, White Oak Road, **Strasburg**, (717) 687-6207

Yogi Bear's Jellystone Park, 340 Blackburn Road, **Quarryville**, (717) 786-3458 or (888) 886-5496, www.jellystonepa.com

Farm Homes

Ben Mar Farm B&B, 5721 Old Philadelphia Pike (Route 340), (717) 768-3309, www.pamall.net/benmar

Cedar Hill Farm B&B, 305 Longenecker Rd., **Mount Joy,** (717) 653-4655 or (717) 653-9242, cedarhill@supernet.com, www.cedarhillfarm.com

Cherry-Crest Farm, 150 Cherry Hill Rd., **Ronks**, (717) 687-6843 www.cherrycrestfarm.com

Country Gardens Farm B&B, 506 Rock Point Road, **Mount Joy,** (717) 426-3316, www.metrocast.com/countrygardens

Country Log House Farm, 1175 Flory Road, **Mount Joy,** (717) 653-4477, www.pamall.net/clhf

Country Pines Farm and Cottage, 1101 Auction Road, **Manheim**, (717) 665-5478

Country View PA B&B, 5463 Old Philadelphia Pike (Route 340), **Kinzers**, (717) 768-0936, www.countryviewpa.com

Eby's Farm B&B, 345 Belmont Road, **Gordonville**, (717) 768-3615, www.ebyfarm.n3.net

Equestrian Estates Horse Farm B&B, 221 Shultz Road, **Willow Street**, (717) 464-2164, www.equestrianbnb.com

Green Acres Farm B&B, 1382 Pinkerton Road, **Mount Joy,** (717) 653-4028, green@redrose.net, www.thegreenacresfarm.com

Iron Stone Acres, 344 South Pool Forge Road, **Narvon**, (717) 354-8547

Jonde Lane Farm, 1103 Auction Road, **Manheim**, (717) 665-4231, www.pamall.net/jondelane

Landis Farm, 2048 Gochlan Road, **Manheim**, (717) 898-7028, www.landisfarm.com

Maple Lane Farm B&B, 505 Paradise Lane, **Paradise**, (717) 687-7479, www.bbdirectory.com/inn/0365.html

Meadow Valley Farm Guest House, 221 Meadow Valley Road, **Ephrata**, (877) 562-4530 or (717) 733-8390

Meadow View K Farm Guest House, 612 Eby Chiques Road, **Mount Joy**, (717) 653-9793, www.meadowviewkfarm.com

Neffdale Farm, 604 Strasburg Road, **Paradise**, (717) 687-7837, www.800padutch.com/neffdale.html

Olde Fogie Farm, 106 Stackstown Road, **Marietta**, (717) 426-3992 or (877) 653-3644, www.oldefogiefarm.com

Olde Stone Guesthouse, 1599 Swan Road, **Atglen**, (610) 593-5572 or (888) 642-9107, www.oldestoneguesthouse.com

Old Summer House B&B, 1294 Weaverland Road, **East Earl**, (717) 445-8422, www.800padutch.com/oldsummer.htm

Penn's Valley Farm and Inn, 6182 Metzler Road, **Manheim**, (717) 898-7386, www.pennsvalleyfarm.com

Pleasant Grove Farm B&B, 368 Pilottown Road, **Peach Bottom**, (717) 548-3100, www.pleasantgrovefarm.com

Rayba Acres Farm, 183 Black Horse Road, **Paradise**, (717) 687-6729, www.800padutch.com/rayba.html

Rocky Acre Farm B&B, 1020 Pinkerton Road, **Mount Joy**, (717) 653-4449, www.rockyacre.com

Runnymede Farm Guest House B&B, 1030 Robert Fulton Highway (Route 222 South), **Quarryville**, (717) 786-3625

Starlit Acres Amish Farm B&B, 4021 B Old Philadelphia Pike, **Gordonville**, (717) 768-3774

Stone Haus Farm B&B, 360 South Esbenshade Road, **Manheim**, (717) 653-8444

Verdant View Farm, 429 Strasburg Road, **Paradise**, (717) 687-7353 or (888) 321-8119, www.verdantview.com

Vogt Farm B&B, 1225 Colebrook Road, **Mount Joy**, (717) 653-4810 or (800) 854-0399, www.vogtfarmbnb.com

Walnut Hill Farm B&B, 801 Walnut Hill Road, **Millersville**, (717) 872-2283 or (888) 746-3417, www.walnuthillfarmbandb.com

Bed and Breakfasts

Lancaster County Bed & Breakfast Inns Association, www.padutchinns.com

Adamstown Inn, 62 West Main Street, **Adamstown**, (717) 484-0800 or (800) 594-4808, www.adamstown.com

Apple Bin Inn, 2835 Willow Street Pike, **Willow Street**, (800) 338-4296 or (717) 464-5881, www.applebininn.com

Artist's Inn and Gallery, 117 East Main Street, **Terre Hill**, (888) 999-4479 or (717) 445-0219, www.artistinn.com

E.J. Bowman House, 2672 Lititz Pike, **Lancaster**, (877) 519-1776 or (717) 519-0808, www.ejbowmanhouse.com

Churchtown Inn, 2100 Main Street, **Churchtown**, (800) 637-4446 or (717) 445-7794, www.churchtowninn.com

Columbian, 360 Chestnut Street, **Columbia**, (800) 422-5869 or (717) 684-5869, www.columbianinn.com

Flowers and Thyme Bed and Breakfast, 238 Strasburg Pike, **Lancaster**, PA 17602, (717) 393-1460, www.members.aol.com/padutchbnb

Gardens of Eden B&B, 1894 Eden Road, **Lancaster**, (717) 393-5179, www.gardens-of-eden.com

Folk Craft Center Bed and Breakfast, 441 Mt. Sidney Road, **Witmer**, (866) 397-3676 or (717) 397-3676, www.folkcraftcenter.com

Harvest Moon Bed and Breakfast, 311 East Main Street, **New Holland**, (717) 354-0213, www.harvestmoonbandb.com

Hillside Farm Bed and Breakfast, 607 Eby Chiques Road, **Mount Joy**, (888) 249-3406 or (717) 653-6697, www.hillsidefarmbandb.com

White Horse Inn, White Horse

Kimmell House Bed and Breakfast, 851 South State Street, **Ephrata**, (800) 861-3385 or (717) 738-3555, www.kimmellhouse.com

King's Cottage, 1049 East King Street, **Lancaster**, (800) 747-8717 or (717) 397-1017, www.kingscottagebb.com

Limestone Inn, 33 East Main Street, **Strasburg**, (800) 278-8392 or (717) 687-8392, www.thelimestoneinn.com

Lovelace Manor Bed and Breakfast, 2236 Marietta Avenue, **Lancaster**, (717) 399-3275 or (866) 713-6384

Mount Gretna Inn, 16 Kauffman Avenue, **Mount Gretna**, (800) 277-6602 or (717) 964-3234, www.mtgretna.com

New Life Homestead B&B, 1400 East King Street, **Lancaster**, (717) 396-8928 or (888) 503-2987

O'Flaherty's Dingeldein House, 1105 East King Street,

Artists Inn, Terre Hill

Lancaster, (800) 779-7765 or (717) 293-1723, www.dingeldein-house.com

Osceola Mill House, 313 Osceola Mill Road, **Gordonville**, (717) 768-3758 or (800) 878-7719, www.lancaster-inn.com

Rocking Horse Bed and Breakfast, 285 West Main Street, **New Holland**, (800) 208-9156 or (717)354-8674, www.rockinghorsebb.com

Rose Manor, 124 South Linden Street, **Manheim**, (800) 666-4932, www.rosemanor.net

Swiss Woods, 500 Blantz Road, **Lititz**, (800) 594-8018 or (717) 627-3358, www.swisswoods.com

Let's Do Lancaster

Every destination has its list of must-see attractions. You haven't done New Orleans if you haven't visited the French Quarter. You haven't done Philadelphia if you haven't seen the Liberty Bell, and you haven't done Chicago if you haven't been to Wrigley Field.

If you want to do Lancaster, your list begins with going to market. For hundreds of years, Lancastrians have been "going to market" to shop for food and socialize with friends. The county has many markets, and at the top of the must-visit list is Lancaster's Central Market, the nation's oldest continuously operating public market house, located on Penn Square, in the center of the city. The current market house has been in operation since 1889, and the first market house on the site opened in the 1730s.

Going to market is both a shopping and a social experience. The stands don't have express lanes, and customers spend as much time talking as shopping. Everyone seems to enjoy the market's leisurely pace of shopping and the variety of accessible goods. Produce fresh from the farm is the top draw, and all sorts of foods are available, so are some nonfood items, such as Amish quilts, books, and baskets.

Central Market is open Tuesdays, Fridays, and Saturdays, beginning around 6 A.M., although some stands really aren't

Philadelphia Pike (Route 340), Intercourse, (800) 390-8436, www.craftsoftheworld.cc

• **Strasburg RailRoad Shops**—In addition to running the tourist trains, the Strasburg RailRoad provides an excellent shopping opportunity for train lovers. Thomas and Friends merchandise, railroad books, hats, model trains, and clothing are all on sale here. Route 741 East, Strasburg, (717) 687-7686, www.strasburgrailroadstore.com

• **1754 Checkerboard House**—This old house is worth seeing, and you can do a little antique shopping in a less hectic atmosphere than the one you'll find in Adamstown. From Lititz, go north on Route 501 and east on Route 322. Reifsnyder Road is the second road on the right. The 1754 Checkerboard House is the first house on the left. Reifsnyder Road, Brickerville, (717) 627-5212

• **Weaver's Dry Goods**—Serious quilters come here for fabrics and other supplies. From Lititz, go north on 501. At the bottom of a long hill, turn left on West Brubaker Valley Road. 108 West Brubaker Valley Road, Lititz, (717) 627-1724

• **Eldreth Pottery**—Eldreth Pottery makes and sells salt-glazed stoneware and redware. 246 North Decatur Street (Route 896), Strasburg, (717) 687-8445, www.eldrethpottery. com

Quilts

Quilt-making is both a practical and an artistic activity for Amish and Mennonite women in Lancaster County. They make quilts in many designs and sell them to supplement their farm incomes. Quilting bees are also a social function.

At many farms you'll see signs that simply say Quilts. When the weather is good, you'll see quilts hanging on wash lines, inviting you to stop and buy them.

All the quilts that you'll see on the farm are handmade, which means that they take many hours to create. Here are some shops that make and sell quilts.

open until 7:30. By 2 P.M., most of the good food is gone, and most of the action is over. The best day to visit is Friday. The crowds are busiest on Friday, and on Saturday, some stand-holders don't come in. They have to operate both their farm or business and their market stand, and they just don't have enough time to come to market three days a week.

One of the most interesting stands at market is Long's Horseradish. Long's is a Lancaster tradition, and your nose will lead you to the stand, where the owner gets customers' attention by grinding horseradish with a fan at his back.

As Lancaster's population has diversified, so have the stands at market. Once, market was essentially an outlet store for farmers. Today, it's that and much more. You'll find foods from Lancaster County and flavors from many parts of the world. On the south side of the building are tables and chairs where people can sit and eat. Market is a favorite place for Lancastrians to find food and friends. If your town doesn't have a market, a visit to Lancaster's Central Market will make you wish that it did.

Merchants at Central Market, Lancaster

Other Must-Do Activities in Lancaster

• For urban dwellers, photographing **cows** is a favorite pastime. Locals shake their heads in amusement when they see people standing by the side of the road, looking at cows and snapping pictures, but it's a popular activity. If you want to take pictures of cows, just take a drive down any rural road. Cows are common on them.

• Driving through a **covered bridge** is another favorite activity for visitors. To find one, see chapter 8.

• Seeing a **buggy** on the roads is also a must for a visit to Lancaster County, and if you travel any road in the eastern part of the county other than Route 30, you'll see buggies.

• Riding the Rails—The **Strasburg RailRoad** is the busiest tourist line in the continental United States, and taking a ride won't take up an entire day. The basic ride is 9 miles through Amish farmlands and lasts about 45 minutes. The railroad is on Route 741 East, Strasburg. For information, call (717) 687-7522 or visit www.strasburgrailroad.com.

Strasburg RailRoad

• For an experience that you won't find everywhere, visit **Buck Motorsports Park.** Tractor pulls, monster-truck shows, and an evening in rural America await you. The park is 10 miles south of Lancaster, and the shows take place on Saturdays at 7 P.M. from May through September. Route 272, Buck, (717) 284-2139, www.buckmotorsports.com.

• For a true taste of Lancaster that you can take home, stop at **Hammond's Pretzel Bakery,** where they roll all their pretzels by hand. The aroma that greets you upon entering will make the visit instantly worthwhile. These are the pretzels that the locals eat, and the company has developed a large mail-order business for fans in faraway places, so if you find yourself hooked, you'll always be able to get your twist. 716 South West End Avenue, Lancaster, (717) 392-7532, www.hammondpretzels.com.

• For outstanding adventures in gluttony, visit a smorgasbord. A smorgasbord is a restaurant with an all-you-can-eat menu, and Lancaster has a few of them. **Miller's** on Route 30 has long been popular with local people. Another popular smorgasbord is **Plain and Fancy Farm** on Route 340, as is **Willow Valley** on Route 272 in Willow Street. **Shady Maple** on Route 23 in Blue Ball is popular with the locals and draws fewer tourists than the others.

When you stop in, don't expect to float out. Pennsylvania Dutch cooking does not feature brown rice and tofu, and you'll leave with a full feeling. You don't need reservations, but they can be a good idea during busy seasons.

• **Mud sales**—No, they don't actually sell mud, but the sales often take place on muddy ground. Mud sales are fund-raisers for volunteer fire companies in Lancaster County, and the most famous takes place at the Gordonville Fire Company on the second Saturday in March. People donate items, and Amish women make quilts to sell. Many Amish men are members of volunteer fire companies in Lancaster County, and these sales draw big crowds and raise lots of money.

Lancaster County has about half a dozen such sales. Most take place in February and March, when farmers aren't as busy as they are during the growing and harvest seasons. **Gordonville Fire Company,** Old Leacock Road, Gordonville, (717) 768-3869 (For information on more sales, go to www.800padutch.com.)

Places Your Friends Won't Discover without This Book

• To get a look at the bounty of Lancaster County, pay a visit to the **Leola Produce Auction** in July or August. This place will give you a pleasant story to relate when you get home. Farmers bring their harvests to the auction to sell to wholesale buyers, and most of the farmers are Amish and Mennonites who bring their products in horse-drawn wagons, often accompanied by their barefoot children.

Individuals don't buy stuff here, unless you're looking for 100

Horses in pasture

dozen ears of corn, but you can sample the melons, and it's intriguing to see wagons filled with corn, tomatoes, melons, and many other produce items. The auction is open from April through October, but summer is definitely the best time to visit. The auction starts at 9 A.M. but not every day of the week and never on Sunday. For the current schedule, call (717) 656-9592. Brethren Church Road, north of Route 23, Leola.

• For **tomatoes,** head to **Washington Boro.** Located beside the Susquehanna River, Washington Boro has a climate that's conducive to growing tomatoes and a local reputation as the source of the earliest tomatoes. One farmer explained that the regions along the river have ten extra growing days at both ends of the season.

The county's first tomatoes usually come from Washington Boro and merit a front-page story in the local paper. The **Tomato Barn** on Route 999, about half a mile east of the river, is a good place to make a purchase, beginning around June 20.

• For a true Lancaster County experience, try **tubing** at **Sickman's Mill.** Tubing means floating down a creek in a big inner tube, like the ones that fill truck tires or even bigger. For Lancaster County residents, tubing usually involves the Pequea Creek in the southwestern part of the county. Sickman's Mill rents tubes and has a campground. 671 Sand Hill Road, Pequea, (717) 872-5951.

Meet Me at the Fair

The county fair is a tradition in rural Pennsylvania. Farmers bring their wares to the fairgrounds, and everyone gets together to have a good time. Curiously, Lancaster County doesn't have a county fair, but many communities have their own fairs. Some take place at the fairgrounds, and some turn a town's streets into a fairground.

Fair season in Lancaster begins with the Elizabethtown Fair in late August and concludes with the Manheim Fair during the second week of October.

For information on all Pennsylvania fairs, visit www.pafairs.org.

Denver Fair (717) 336-4072—second week of September
Elizabethtown Fair (717) 367-7256—late August
Ephrata Fair (717) 733-4451—late September
Manheim Community Farm Show (717) 361-0998—second week of October
New Holland Farmers Fair (717) 354-5880—first week of October
Southern Lancaster County Fair Quarryville (717) 786-1054—mid-September
West Lampeter Community Fair Lampeter (717) 687-0351—late September
York Fair (717) 848-2596, info@yorkfair.org—begins the Friday following Labor Day and runs for ten days (It is on a scale much larger than most community fairs. Held on the 120 acres of the York Fairgrounds, it resembles a state fair with famous-named entertainment and tens of thousands of visitors.)

A Cross-Cultural Encounter

It's a summer morning, and the Leola Produce Auction is a busy place. Horse-drawn wagons are backed up to the road, and buyers are eager to take the melons, corn, and tomatoes back to their stores and restaurants.

Churches

Lancaster County's most famous tourist group is a religious group that doesn't have churches. The Amish worship in their homes, but Lancaster County has a wide variety of churches. Most are Christian, but there are also Judaic and Islamic worship centers in the area.

Many churches are old and historical. Among them are

• **Saint James Episcopal** at Duke and Orange streets in downtown Lancaster. Built around 1744, it's seen much of Lancaster's history.

• So has **Trinity Lutheran** in the first block of South Duke Street.

• Bethel African Methodist Episcopal Church on East

Strawberry Street has been around for almost 200 years, and it played a part in the Underground Railroad. (See entry under "Theatre" in chapter 5.)

Around Lancaster County are old churches, new churches, big churches, and small churches. Sometimes they have signs that say things such as Visitors Expected.

You can walk to many of the churches in the city of Lancaster. For directions and a guided walking tour, visit the Downtown Information Center at 100 South Queen Street in Lancaster.

Church in Churchtown

Roadside stand

Roadside stand

A Self-Guided Tour

In these 17 miles, you'll get a good look at many of the things that make Lancaster County attractive to visitors. It takes you through the heart of Amish Country, so be alert for buggies, scooters, and bicycles.

Begin at the Bird-in-Hand Farmers' Market on Route 340.

At the west end of the parking lot, go left on Maple Avenue.

Go right on North Ronks Road.

Go left on Irishtown Road.

Go left on Old Leacock Road.

Go left on Old Philadelphia Pike.

Go right on North Harvest Road.

At stop sign, go right onto Newport Road.

Go left on Scenic Road.

At stop sign, go right and quickly left, staying on Scenic Road.

Go left on Centerville Road.

Go left on Zeltenreich Road.

Go right on Musser School Road.

Go left on Groffdale Road.

Go right on East Eby Road.

Go left on Stumptown Road.

Go left on Monterey Road.

Go left to Miller's Store.*

Return to Monterey Road and go left.

Go right on Church Road.

Go left on Ronks Road.

Go right on Old Philadelphia Pike and you'll be back at the Bird-in-Hand Farmers' Market.

* Miller's is optional. It's a health-food store on an Amish farm.

What You'll See: On most of these roads, one Amish farm runs into another. One-room schoolhouses are numerous. On many farms, you'll see roadside stands and signs for items, such as quilts and furniture.

The Gordonville Fire Company is home to the most popular of the fire company auctions or mud sales, popular in Lancaster County.

At the intersection of Newport and Stumptown roads is a little park beside the creek. Across the road is the Mascot Roller Mill, a free attraction that shows how millers turned grains into flour.

This tour is ideal for bicyclists. Traffic is light, and hills are minimal.

Lancaster County Attractions

The attractions in Lancaster County fall broadly into seven different general categories: the Amish people, history and museums, trains, shopping centers and antique stores, theatre, amusing places for children, and food. Here is detailed information on such attractions.

The Amish People

It's easy to look at the Amish. If you want to learn more about them, try these places:

• Amish Mennonite Information Center, Route 340, Intercourse, (717) 768-0807

• Mennonite Information Center, 2209 Millstream Road, Lancaster (beside Route 30), (717) 299-0954, www.mennonite-infoctr.com

• Amish Country Homestead, Route 340, between Bird-in-Hand and Intercourse, (717) 768-3600 (See how the Amish live in this nine-room house.)

• Amish Farm and House, 2395 Lincoln Highway (Route 30 East), Lancaster, (717) 394-6185, www.amishfarmandhouse.com (Tour this house, which dates to 1805, and the 25-acre, working farm.)

• The Amish Village, Route 896 North, Strasburg, (717)

687-8511, www.800padutch.com\avillage.html (Get a look at many aspects of Amish life here, including home, farm, and school.)

• The People's Place, Route 340, in the heart of downtown Intercourse, (800) 390-8436, www.thepeoplesplace.com (A movie short called *Who Are the Amish?* is a highlight here, as is an extensive bookstore with many titles about the Amish and Mennonites.)

History and Museums

Lancaster County is big on American history. Here are some of the important contributions that have come from Lancaster:

• **Driving on the right**—The rest of the world drives on the other side of the road. Americans drive on the right because of a Lancaster County invention. The Conestoga wagon carried hundreds of thousands of settlers west, and it takes its name from the Conestoga Valley of Lancaster County, where it originated. Because the builders of Conestoga wagons put the driver's seat on the left side of the wagon, Americans now drive on the right side of the road. You can see Conestoga wagons at the Bird-in-Hand Farmers' Market and at Kitchen Kettle Village in Intercourse.

• **Kentucky rifle**—Despite the name, this gun, which was instrumental in conquering the American wilderness, was a Pennsylvania product. It gained the Kentucky name from frontiersmen who took it there, but it came from Pennsylvania, including Lancaster County.

• **America's First Turnpike**—Opened in 1794, it linked Lancaster and Philadelphia. Today, the Lancaster County portion of the road is the Old Philadelphia Pike, Route 340.

• **Pennsylvania's Only President**—James Buchanan lived at Wheatland, just west of Lancaster.

• **Lancaster-York Heritage Region**—Heritage Tourism is a new initiative that celebrates the joint history of Lancaster and

York counties. As of autumn 2002, the plan was close to fruition. Its highlight will be the Lower Susquehanna Water Trail, which will detail the historical activities along the Susquehanna from Harrisburg to the Maryland border. As a result of all its history, Lancaster County has a long list of museums. Many focus on the people and events of Lancaster County, and a few have less obvious connections to Lancaster. For an Internet tour of the museums, go to www.lancastercountymuseums.org.

• **Railroad Museum of Pennsylvania**—This museum tells the story of railroading in Pennsylvania. Everything has a Pennsylvania connection. Museum displays consist of things that were manufactured here or people who served on railroads in Pennsylvania. Historic, restored locomotives and cars are the most impressive pieces in the collection. Route 741 East, Strasburg, (717) 687-8628, www.rrmuseumpa.org

• **National Toy Train Museum**—The headquarters of the Train Collectors Association, it's a great place to see toy trains in action. 300 Paradise Lane, just off Route 741 East, Strasburg, (717) 687-8976, www.traincollectors.org

• **Landis Valley Museum**—This museum tells the story of Pennsylvania Dutch life in Lancaster County in a historic village with craftsmen and animals. A highlight is the Heirloom Seed Project, which keeps alive crop varieties grown by Pennsylvania Dutch settlers. Route 272, north of Lancaster, (717) 569-0401, www.landisvalleymuseum.org

• **Ephrata Cloister**—Long before the hippies of the 1960s revived the idea of communal living, it was happening in Ephrata in the eighteenth century. Many buildings are still standing. 632 W. Main Street, Ephrata, (717) 733-6600, www.phmc.state.pa.us

• **Wheatland**—The home of Pres. James Buchanan, Wheatland is an outstanding example of Federal architecture. 1120 Marietta Avenue, Lancaster, (717) 392-8271, www.wheatland.org

Landis Valley Museum, Lancaster

• **Lancaster County Historical Society**—The society houses Lancaster artifacts and an extensive collection of books and documents that detail Lancaster's history. 230 North President Avenue, Lancaster, adjacent to Wheatland, (717) 392-4633, www.lanclio.org

• **National Watch and Clock Museum**—From pocket watches to grandfather clocks, the museum tracks the history of timepieces and clock making. 514 Poplar Street, Columbia, (717) 684-8261, www.nawcc.org

• **American Military Edged Weaponry Museum**—This museum displays military artifacts as well as items from many different wars, including the Spanish-American War, WWI, WWII, the

Korean War, and Viet Nam. 3562 Old Philadelphia Pike (Route 340), Intercourse, (717) 768-7185

• **North Museum of Natural History and Science**—The museum has a planetarium, snakes, and exhibits on natural history and archaeology. 400 College Avenue, Lancaster, (717) 291-3941, www.northmuseum.org

• **Heritage Center Museum**—This free museum displays exhibits of local history, highlighting furniture, quilts, Amish art, and folk art. Penn Square, downtown Lancaster, (717) 299-6440, www.lancasterheritage.com

• **Lancaster Museum of Art**—Housed in a Greek Revival mansion, the museum focuses on exhibits of contemporary art. It is in Musser Park, a pleasant little city park. 135 North Lime Street, Lancaster, (717) 394-3497, www.lancastermuseum-art.com

• **Rock Ford Plantation**—This 1794 Georgian mansion was the home of Gen. Edward Hand, an important figure in the American Revolution who became adjutant general of the Continental Army under Gen. George Washington. 881 Rock Ford Road, Lancaster, (717) 392-7223, www.rockfordplanta-tion.org

• **Conestoga Area Historical Society**—The museum follows the history of southwestern Lancaster County in buildings that date from the eighteenth century. 51 Kendig Road, Conestoga, (717) 872-1699, www.rootsweb.com/~pacahs/cahs.htm

• **Hans Herr House**—This is the oldest building in Lancaster County and the oldest Mennonite meeting house in America, dating to 1719. 1849 Hans Herr Drive, Willow Street, (717) 464-4438, www.hansherr.org

• **Wright's Ferry Museum**—Built in 1738, this large stone home contains a large collection of early-eighteenth-century Philadelphia furniture and English accessories predating 1750. Second and Cherry streets, Columbia, (717) 684-4325

Hans Herr House, Willow Street

Trains

Lancaster County has a long and distinguished railroad history. For many years, Lancaster was a busy stop on the Pennsylvania Railroad, and today it's still a busy station on Amtrak's Philadelphia/Harrisburg line. A century ago, train tracks ran through every part of Lancaster County, and the National Railway Historical Society had its beginnings in Lancaster in 1933. Today, passenger and freight trains run through Lancaster County every day, and from the grounds of Conestoga Valley High School, it's possible to see trains running on two different lines—a fairly busy freight line and Amtrak's Philadelphia/Harrisburg line.

For rail fans, the small town of Strasburg is a mandatory place to visit. Before the Strasburg RailRoad grew into its status as the busiest tourist railroad in the continental U.S.A., it was a working freight line, and it dates back to 1832. Today,

Strasburg bills itself Traintown, U.S.A., and it offers visitors the Strasburg RailRoad; the Railroad Museum of Pennsylvania; the Red Caboose Motel, where all the rooms are converted cabooses; the Toy Train Museum; and a variety of shops that sell train books, clothing, memorabilia, and toy trains.

Shopping/Antiques

Lancaster, Pennsylvania, was voted **Best Shopping Destination for Groups** in *Destinations* magazine's (publication of the American Bus Association) 2002 annual survey. That ranking is a strong endorsement of one of Lancaster's newer attractions— shopping. Retailers have followed the tourists to Lancaster County, and shopping is now a major attraction. Outlet shopping began in nearby Reading, and now it's big in Lancaster.

The shopping sites that attract most groups are the two large outlet centers along Route 30. Tanger Outlet Center, (800) 408-3477, www.tangeroutlet.com, has more than 60 stores. Rockvale Square, (717) 293-9595, www.rockvalesquareoutlets.com, has more than 100 stores.

Those outlets are hardly the only shopping attractions, and from the big malls to quaint quilt shops on Amish farms to downtown Lancaster to the antiques shops in Adamstown, shoppers find excellent opportunities to buy, buy, buy.

The shopping places that offer the most merchants and the most variety are Lancaster County's two large flea markets.

• **Root's Country Market and Auction**—Root's is a place to buy almost everything. Produce, clothing, collectibles, and much more are available every Tuesday. Root's is both a place to shop and socialize. 705 Graystone Road, Manheim, (717) 898-7811, www.rootsmarket.com (from Route 72, south of the borough of Manheim, look for the signs)

• **Green Dragon Market and Auction**—Like Root's, Green Dragon is a place where you can buy almost anything. Hours of operation are on Fridays, and it's usually a busy place. The best

Everywhere a sign

way to find it is to follow Route 272 north of Ephrata and to look for the big Green Dragon sign. 955 North State Street, Ephrata, (717) 738-1117, www.greendragonmarket.com

Some other interesting places to shop include

• **300 block of North Queen Street**—This block offers a quirky collection of shops that sell antiques, used bicycles, jewelry, and old clothing. It's also home to America's oldest Goodyear tire dealer. Downtown Lancaster

• **Riehl's Quilts and Crafts**—Located on a working Amish farm, this shop sells quilts and pillows directly from the home, and they take VISA and MasterCard. 247 East Eby Road, Leola, (717) 656-0697

• **Sam's Steins and Collectibles**—American and German steins, clocks, signs, and glasses fill this shop. 2207 Lincoln Highway East (Route 30), Lancaster, (717) 394-6404

• **Witmer Quilt Shop**—More than 150 quilts in various sizes

Hex signs

and patterns are on display here. 1070 West Main Street (Route 23), New Holland, (717) 656-9526

• **Jacob Zook's Original Hex Signs**—Hex signs are part of the Pennsylvania Dutch heritage. They adorn barns to bring good luck or just to look pretty. Smaller ones are common decorations in homes. Route 30 East, Paradise, (717) 687-9329, www.hexsigns.com

• **Ten Thousand Villages**—The store offers pottery, jewelry, baskets, rugs, and much more from many parts of the world. The Oriental Rug Room carries Persians, dhurries, and other hand-knotted rugs. The income from these operations subsequently returns to more than 30 countries. 240 North Reading Road (Route 272), Ephrata, (717) 721-8400, www.tenthousandvillages. com

• **Crafts of the World**—This is a branch of Ten Thousand Villages, located in a spot with more foot traffic. 3518 Old

• **Riehl's Quilts and Crafts,** 247 East Eby Road, Leola, (717) 656-0697

• Quilt shop at **Miller's Smorgasbord,** Route 30, 1 mile east of Route 896, Ronks, (717) 687-8480, ext. 49

• **Witmer's Quilt Shop,** 1070 West Main Street, New Holland, (717) 656-9526

• **Sylvia Petersheim's Quilts and Crafts,** 2544 Old Philadelphia Pike (Route 340), Bird-in-Hand, (717) 392-6404

• **Village Quilts,** Kitchen Kettle Village, Intercourse, (717) 768-0783, www.kitchenkettle.com/quilts

• **The Old Country Store,** 3510 Old Philadelphia Pike, Intercourse, (800) 828-8218, www.theoldcountrystore.com

Theatre

We're #3!

That may not sound like much, but it's an impressive, and perhaps unlikely, distinction for Lancaster County's tourism business. According to the 2002 survey by *Destinations* magazine, a publication of the American Bus Association, Sight and Sound Millenium Theatre in Strasburg ranked third in the Best Theater/Entertainment for Groups category, preceded by Broadway and Branson, Missouri.

• **Sight and Sound Millennium Theatre** is a modern theatre that produces stories of the Bible, such as Daniel, and the *Miracle of Christmas* on stage. The theatre has 2,000 seats and a 300-foot, wraparound stage. The sound and the effects are spectacular, and the fans pour in. The current theatre is a bigger and better replacement for the one that burned down in the 1998. While the theatre was down, tourism dropped off significantly, especially group tours. Now, Sight and Sound Millennium Theatre is the biggest theatre attraction in Lancaster County, but it's hardly the only one.

Fulton Opera House, downtown Lancaster

• Just north of Sight and Sound Millennium Theatre on Route 896 is **Sight and Sound Living Waters Theatre,** which also produces biblical shows but does so in a smaller theatre. These places are very popular, so it's wise to call ahead for tickets. In addition to the actual shows, the Millennium Theatre offers 75-minute tours of the production facilities. Route 896, north of Strasburg, (717) 687-7800, www.bibleonstage.com

• Lancaster's oldest and most elegant theatre is the **Fulton Opera House** at 12 North Prince Street in downtown Lancaster. The Fulton has been around for more than 150 years, and when Lancastrians dress up to go to the theatre, they're probably going to the Fulton. It's the kind of place in which it's easy to imagine horse-drawn carriages arriving on snowy nights to discharge ladies in long dresses and men in top hats.

The name honors Robert Fulton, a Lancaster County native credited with the invention of the steamboat. When it opened in 1852, the large Italianate structure quickly became the city's cultural center. A week after it opened, the first big show featured Ole Bull, a famous Norwegian violinist, and a youthful soprano named Adelina Patti who became the most celebrated soprano in the world during the second half of the nineteenth century. In 1852, she was all of nine years old.

The Fulton produces shows such as *The King and I, My Fair Lady,* and *The Sound of Music.* It's also home to the Lancaster Symphony Orchestra. (717) 394-7133, www.fultontheatre.org

• **Playhouse in the Park**—It's small and cozy, and the performances are good. The Playhouse in the Park is a place to enjoy a fine performance in a relaxed atmosphere. Cocalico Street, Ephrata, (717) 733-7966, www.ephrataplayhouseinthe-park.org

• **Gretna Theatre**—Mount Gretna is a pleasant little place that began as a summer resort in the 1880s. One of the highlights is the Gretna Theatre, which puts on stage shows and musical performances. The current theatre replaced the old one, which collapsed under the weight of heavy snow in the 1990s. Route 117 at Timbers Road, Mount Gretna, (717) 964-3627, www.mtgretna.com/theatre

• **Dutch Apple Dinner Theatre**—Dinner at 6 P.M. and show at 8 P.M. is the menu at Dutch Apple. 510 Centerville Road, Lancaster, (717) 898-1900, www.dutchapple.com

• **American Music Theatre**—Famous singers and musicians grace the stage of this modern theatre. 2425 Lincoln Highway East, Lancaster, (800) 648-4102, www.americanmusictheatre.com

• **Rainbow Dinner Theatre**—All comedy, all the time is the theme at Rainbow. Route 30 East, Paradise, (800) 292-4301 or (717) 299-4300, rainbowdinnertheatre.com

CH. BERGAMASCO  S.ᵗ PETERSBOURG

Adelina Patti

• **Living the Experience**—Lancaster County was an important part of the Underground Railroad, and Bethel African Methodist Episcopal Church, founded in 1817, was a station on the line. Today, the church presents a stage show called *Living the Experience,* which shows what life was like during the time of the Underground Railroad. The show also includes a meal similar to what people would have eaten then. 450 East Strawberry Street, Lancaster, (717) 396-8381, www.livingtheundergroundrailroad.com

Living the Experience, Bethel AME Church, Lancaster

Water ride at HersheyPark

Fun for Children

Family Fun magazine, in its 2001 readers' survey, placed Lancaster, Pennsylvania, as its second-place winner (first place was Bar Harbor, Maine) in the category of Top Tourist Town Picks, Northeast Region. The results of that survey are evidence that Lancaster County doesn't ignore the children. The county has many good attractions for children and several that are exclusively for children, including an amusement park.

• **Dutch Wonderland Amusement Park**'s advertising describes the park as "a kingdom for kids." The description is accurate, and kids and adults will enjoy a visit to an amusement park where the rides don't try to separate riders from their stomachs. Everything is on a smaller and slower scale here than at the bigger parks, and the lack of high-speed rides has one interesting effect: few teenagers come to this park. It really is a family place where grandparents, parents, and children can enjoy the rides together.

Amazing Maize Maze, Strasburg

In 2001, Hershey Entertainment and Resorts Company (HERCO), which also operates HersheyPark, purchased Dutch Wonderland. For the 2002 season, HERCO added new rides and did extensive upgrades to the park. 2249 Route 30 East, Lancaster, (717) 291-1888, www.dutchwonderland.com

• The **Strasburg RailRoad**'s hulking steam locomotives make the eyes of any child open wide. The Strasburg is the busiest tourist railroad in the continental United States, and its regular rides are only 45 minutes long, which is ideal for children. The rides also offer the option of taking a picnic lunch, getting off at a grove along the route, and catching a later train back. Children enjoy playing on the swings and playground equipment at the grove, and in summer, it's only half an hour between trains. Another option is to get off at the grove, cross the road, and do the Amazing Maize Maze. (See description in this chapter.)

Thomas the Tank Engine is a regular visitor to the Strasburg RailRoad, and he even receives repairs in the shop there. His

Hands-On House, Lancaster

presence always draws big crowds, so if you want to see Thomas, it's a good idea to purchase tickets in advance. Route 741 East, Strasburg, (717) 687-7522, www.strasburgrailroad.com

• **Amazing Maize Maze**—Get lost in a cornfield. Cherry Crest Farm plants more than five acres of corn in a maze pattern, and the challenge is to find your way out. Also on the farm are a petting zoo, hayrides, and other fun farm events. The maze opens around Independence Day, which is the time when the corn reaches sufficient height to make the maze challenging. 150 Cherry Hill Road, Ronks, (717) 687-6843, www.cherrycrestfarm.com (*Note:* Despite the address, this attraction is actually close to Strasburg. It's right beside the tracks of the Strasburg RailRoad, and Cherry Hill Road runs between Route 741 and the village of Paradise.)

• At the **National Toy Train Museum** children can enjoy extensive displays of model trains. The museum is just down the tracks from the Strasburg RailRoad station, and it's the headquarters of the Train Collectors Association, an organization dedicated to preserving historic toy trains. Five operating layouts are on display, and visitors can learn about toy trains from continuously running videos. 300 Paradise Lane, Strasburg, (717) 687-8976, www.traincollectors.org

• It's a curious thing that the word *museum* is included in the name of the **Hands-On House Children's Museum** in Lancaster because this is not a place filled with stationary displays. It's actually a very active and interactive place. Children learn by doing, and at the Hands-On House, adults and children ages two to ten play together and learn together. The exhibits, classes, and programs feature interactive activities, and they operate on the theory that children will learn more if learning is fun. 721 Landis Valley Road, (717) 569-KIDS, www.handsonhouse.org

• **Hole in the Wall Puppet Theatre** produces stage shows, such as *The Wizard of Oz* and *Dr. Dolittle*, using puppets. The small building was once a home in downtown Lancaster, and the first four rows of seats are just for children. 126 North Water Street, Lancaster, (717) 394-8398, www.holeinthe-wallpuppettheatre.com

Food

Ultimately, Lancaster County is all about food. According to the Pennsylvania Farm Bureau in 2002, Lancaster County is Pennsylvania's most productive agricultural county, generating more than $725 million annually from 5,910 farms. Most of that number comes from cows and chickens, but produce production is increasing steadily.

In Lancaster County, the eating opportunities are numerous, and they've become more varied as the county's population has diversified. In addition to Pennsylvania Dutch smorgasbords, the county now has restaurants that offer flavors from many nations.

Sturgis Pretzel Bakery, Lititz

Once, the only flavors available were those from Pennsylvania and Dutch, but now you can find food from places such as China, India, Thailand, Viet Nam, England, Italy, France, Mexico, and Jamaica. Each week, the Nav Jiwan International Tea Room at Ten Thousand Villages in Ephrata features the foods of a different country. So while Lancaster County certainly doesn't offer as many dining options as New York City, you do have choices.

In addition to restaurants, Lancaster County offers food in other formats. The county is a big producer of snack foods, and roadside stands give visitors an opportunity to buy produce directly from the farm, which means it's fresher than anything you can buy in a store.

Here are some of the brands of snack foods produced in and near Lancaster County:

• **Auntie Anne's Soft Pretzels**—Headquartered in Lancaster County, this company has quickly become an international chain. It has stores in places like Park City Mall.

• **Hammond's Pretzel Bakery**—These are the pretzels favored by locals. 716 South West End Avenue, Lancaster, (717) 392-7532.

• **Sturgis Pretzel Bakery**—America's first pretzel bakery is still producing them. 219 East Main Street, Lititz, (717) 626-4354

• **Herr's Potato Chips**—It's actually in Chester County, but it's close, and the tour is interesting. Route 272, Nottingham, (800) 523-5030

• **Hershey's Chocolate World**—This is in Dauphin County, and it offers an interesting view of the entire process of making chocolate, from the planting of cocoa trees to the manufacturing in Hershey. Hershey, (800) HERSHEY

Like many places, Lancaster County offers some favorite local foods that aren't likely to win approval from cardiologists or dietitians. Among the delights more popular in Lancaster County than elsewhere are

• **Shoo-fly pie**—Despite its name, shoo-fly pie doesn't actually have flies as one of the ingredients, but the name does come from settlers who had to shoo flies away from the sticky sweet concoctions. The main ingredient is molasses, blended with flour and shortening. They bake them from regular ingredients now, but the story is that the original purpose of shoo-fly pies was to use up ingredients, such as molasses and flour, that had lasted through the winter. Shoo-fly pies are a local staple, and you can find them at markets and roadside stands.

• **Red beet eggs**—It's possible that, outside the borders of Lancaster County, no one has ever consumed one of these. If you're in a market or a convenience store and you see eggs of a curious color, you've probably discovered red beet eggs. These are produced by soaking hard-boiled eggs in pickled beet juice. In Lancaster County, they're a popular snack item.

• **Apple fritters**—These are the apple equivalents to French fries. They're slices of apple breaded and deep-fried in oil, and you can find them at outdoor markets and fairs.

• **Funnel cakes**—These cakes are batter funneled into hot oil to create rings around rings. Watching somebody form them is as interesting as eating them, and you'll find funnel cakes at any self-respecting social event in Lancaster County.

• **Fasnachts**—These yeast doughnuts are probably the only food with a day named after them. In Lancaster County, Shrove Tuesday, the day before Ash Wednesday, is Fasnacht Day. Tuesday is a market day, and Central Market overflows with fasnachts, which are deep-fried doughnuts. Usually, they're rectangular with a slit cut into the center.

• **Sauerkraut**—This fermented cabbage dish is a Lancaster County staple, and the section of the city called Cabbage Hill takes part of its name from German settlers who grew cabbages in their small yards.

Pennsylvania Dutch tradition says that eating sauerkraut with pork and mashed potatoes on New Year's Day will bring good fortune for the entire year. Several fire companies have fund-raiser sauerkraut dinners on New Year's Day, and sauerkraut often shows up as an optional topping on hot dogs at football games and at fairs.

• **Root beer**—At many roadside stands on Amish farms, you'll see signs for homemade root beer. In some places, you'll also find birch beer. You can buy it by the cup or by the gallon, and a cold root beer can taste very good on a hot summer day.

• **Potato chips**—The first potato chip was created by accident in Saratoga Springs, New York, in the 1850s, and the snacks quickly found friends in Lancaster County and neighboring counties. If any place can claim to be the potato-chip capital of the world, it's Pennsylvania Dutch Country.

Take a stroll through a local supermarket, and you'll find as many as a dozen brands of chips. Several are store brands and national brands, but most are regional. Made within the undefined borders of Pennsylvania Dutch Country are Stehman's, Zerbe's, Good's, Mumma's, Bickel's, Martin's, Utz's, Gibble's, Middleswarth's, Snyder's, and Herr's. Stop in a local supermarket and you'll see an entire aisle devoted to potato chips.

These companies vary greatly in size. Herr's and Utz's are big ones and you'll see their advertising billboards in baseball stadiums. Stehman's and Zerbe's are small operations with loyal local followings.

No one has a definite explanation of why chips are so popular and such a big business in the area. Potatoes aren't native to the region, and they're not a huge crop now, but potato chips are an important part of life in Pennsylvania Dutch Country.

• **Pretzels**—Just as popular as chips are pretzels, which are also a major regional industry. The city of Reading in Berks County calls itself Pretzel City, and Lititz is home to America's first pretzel bakery, Sturgis, which is still operating.

Pretzels' local popularity may be easier to explain than that of chips. Lancaster County has a heavy German population, and pretzels trace their history to Bavaria, so that connection seems fairly clear.

Among Lancaster County natives, Hammond's pretzels are the most popular, and unconfirmed stories say that a White House chef from Lancaster introduced a former president to Lancaster's favorite twist.

Within Lancaster County, the pretzel-making companies come in various sizes. Anderson's bills itself as the world's largest pretzel bakery, and many of the pretzels that it bakes carry names of stores and celebrities. In contrast, Hammond's rolls each pretzel by hand, and visitors to the bakery can buy them when they're still warm.

• **Malt beverages and spirits**—While some religious groups in Lancaster County have traditionally discouraged the consumption of alcohol, the county has never been a collection of teetotalers. In fact, Lancaster County has a long association with beer and other malt beverages.

Historical records indicate that in 1772, when Lancaster's population was around 2,100, it had as many as 32 taverns. At that time, taverns were more than just places to drink. They were gathering places and community centers, and many towns grew up around them. In Lancaster County, the towns of Bird-in-Hand, Blue Ball, and White Horse take their names from tavern signs. Centuries ago, most people couldn't read, so a sign, such as one with a blue ball, was easy to recognize.

When the Lancaster/Philadelphia Turnpike was a busy place, in the early nineteenth century, it had 62 taverns along its 68 miles.

In the middle of the nineteenth century, Mount Joy carried the title of Malt Beverage Capital of the World. The region grew more corn than the cows could eat, so some local entrepreneurs found other uses for it.

For centuries, the city of Lancaster seemed to have a bar on every corner, especially in the heavily German area called Cabbage Hill, and some of the bars did their own brewing. Rumor has it that during Prohibition a set of pipes running through Lancaster's sewer system carried beer to clandestine bars around the city.

Today, Lancaster County is still producing beer and wine, and the breweries and wineries welcome visitors for tours and tastes.

• **Stoudt Brewing Company**—This brewing company is just one part of Stoudtburg, a complex that includes antique shops and a village modeled on a medieval German village. Stoudtburg sponsors several Microbrew Fests every year. Route 272, Adamstown, (717) 484-4387, www.stoudtsbeer. com

• **Lancaster Brewing Company**—Housed in an old warehouse in the city, Lancaster Brewing Company has a restaurant on site. 302 North Plum Street, Lancaster, (717) 391-6258, www.lancasterbrewing.com

• **Bube's Brewery**—An intact nineteenth-century brewery,

Bube's is home to four different restaurants. 102 North Market Street, Mount Joy, (717) 653-2056, www.bubesbrewery.com

• **Mount Hope Winery**—Mount Hope also hosts the Pennsylvania Renaissance Faire from August through October. PA Route 72 at the Pennsylvania Turnpike, Cornwall, (717) 665-7021, www.parenaissancefaire.com

• **Nissley Vineyards**—Located near the Susquehanna River, Nissley hosts music events on the lawn on summer Saturday evenings. 140 Vintage Drive, Bainbridge, (717) 426-3514, www.nissleywine.com

• **Lancaster County Winery**—799 Rawlinsville Road, Willow Street, (717) 464-3555, www.lancastercountywinery.com

• **Twin Brook Winery**—5697 Strasburg Road, Gap, (717) 442-4915, www.gabrielshill.com

What's Growing Out There

Lancaster County has more than 400,000 acres (625 square miles) in agriculture. Most of that land grows crops, and city people may not recognize everything that's growing out there. (Many Lancaster County residents can't tell the difference between potatoes and soybeans either.)

Farmers in Lancaster County plant four major crops and many other ones: corn, soybeans, alfalfa, and tobacco. Since 1960, the health problems associated with tobacco have led farmers to reduce their production by about 90 percent. As tastes, health concerns, and farm economics change, so do the crops that farmers plant. Sometimes, they wait until the day of planting to decide what to put into the ground. Prices, supplies, and demand influence what goes into the fields.

A crop that many people would like to grow is hemp. Once upon a time, it was the most important crop in the world. People made everything from ropes to clothing from it, but commercial hemp's relation to marijuana led legislators to outlaw hemp production. At one time, hemp was big in Lancaster

County, and the name is still common. Lancaster County, for example, has a Hempfield School District and a Hempland Road. Someday soon, hemp may make a comeback as a commercial crop, but as of 2002 it was still illegal.

Corn is the easiest crop to identify because it's the tallest. Stalks grow to heights of six feet or more, and fields cover many acres. Most of the corn grown in Lancaster County winds up as animal feed, but sweet corn is a local summer favorite.

Soybeans grow much closer to the ground than corn does. The plants reach a height of two feet, and the beans grow in hairy little pods. Soybeans are a staple in China and much of Asia, and in addition to animal feed, they wind up as tofu (bean curd), margarine, and ingredients in hundreds of processed foods.

Alfalfa is a grass that farmers feed to animals, and it usually winds up as hay. It grows to about three or four feet, and if you see a farmer making hay, he's probably cutting alfalfa. In a good year, farmers can get four or five cuttings of alfalfa. Like the grass in a lawn, it continues to grow until the cold weather turns it dormant.

Tobacco plants have many leaves. The plants can grow to about four feet, and most of the tobacco grown in Lancaster County goes into cigars.

In addition to those four crops, the fields of Lancaster County produce just about everything that will grow at 40 degrees north latitude. By mid-July, **tomatoes** are everywhere. If you're buying tomatoes to take home, it's okay to buy some that aren't completely ripe. Tomatoes will ripen after they're off the vine. If they show even a hint of color other than green, they'll eventually ripen. In July, the small town of Washington Boro has its Tomato Festival.

Sweet corn is another local favorite, and the harvesting of the first sweet corn always earns a story in the local papers.

With improvements in genetics and planting techniques, that harvest now comes earlier than ever. The first sweet corn is available by mid-June, and it's available into October.

For decades, Silver Queen corn was as much a part of summer in Lancaster County as thunderstorms and hot weather are, but Silver Queen has practically disappeared, replaced by hybrid varieties such as Argent, Incredible, and Silver King. The new varieties are sweeter, and they remain fresh longer.

If you're buying corn on the cob, look for ears that are big and kernels that are fully filled out. If the kernels have indentation on top, it's an indication that they're old and losing moisture. If you buy corn directly from the farm at a roadside stand, you'll have no concerns about its age.

Corn on the cob is a local favorite, and corn in many forms finds its way into a variety of dishes, such as corn pudding,

Bottom to top: tobacco, soybeans, corn

muffins, fritters, and pies. Chicken corn soup is a local favorite. **Beans** are a common complement for corn. In societies around the world, people have combined grains such as corn with legumes such as beans and peas to form complete proteins. Native Americans made succotash from corn and lima beans. In the Orient, dishes have always included rice and soybeans.

In Lancaster, green and yellow beans are almost always available with corn. Soybeans rarely make it to market in raw form, but once in a while, you'll see them. Compared to other beans, they're less tasty.

Peas are beans' close cousins. Peas grow well in cool weather, while beans favor hot weather. Peas are available in spring and fall. The tastiest are sugar peas.

Celery is big in Lancaster County, and it's available all year. Hodecker's is the name most associated with it. They have a stand at Central Market.

Broccoli and **cauliflower** hit market twice a year, in spring and autumn. Sometimes, at roadside or market stands, you can get a lot of broccoli or cauliflower for a very small price. Cauliflower isn't naturally white. It gets that way because growers tie the leaves over the heads to prevent the formation of color.

Cabbage is a Pennsylvania Dutch staple, and it grows alongside broccoli and cauliflower (they're all cousins) in many fields.

Asparagus is a spring vegetable, and many farms have a patch. Supplies are best in May and almost completely gone by June.

Many varieties of **squash** make their way to market. The most common is zucchini, and a local favorite is pattypan squash. Pattypans are little yellow or white squash in the shape of buttons. **Pumpkins** are close relatives of squash, and you'll see fields filled with both.

The biggest cash crop in Pennsylvania is **mushrooms.** This may come as a surprise, because you'll never see them growing in a field. Well, you may see some mushrooms growing out there, but it's best not to eat them. The commercial mushroom center is near Kennett Square in Chester County, and mushrooms grow inside, under controlled conditions.

Fruits

The Amish Country isn't a major fruit-producing region, but you can still find a nice variety of tree and field fruits. Lancaster County has two fairly large orchards, and you can buy their fruits at the following stores on the properties:

- **Kauffman's**—Route 340, Bird-in-Hand, (717) 768-7112
- **Cherry Hill Orchards**—Route 741 and Long Lane, New Danville, (717) 872-8311 (Cherry Hill offers a pick-your-own option. You can go into the orchards and pick cherries. It's a popular local pastime in June and July.)

Other fruits available at the orchards are **apples, peaches,** and **plums.**

Strawberries show up in late May, and many churches and civic organizations sponsor strawberry festivals.

Cherry Hill Orchards, New Danville

If you'd like to forage for food, look for wild **raspberries** in late June and July. They grow everywhere, usually at the edge of a wooded area. Black raspberries ripen in late June. Red raspberries begin to ripen around July 4, and the season is short, usually lasting no more than two weeks.

Route 322 between Ephrata and the Chester County line has the nickname Cantaloupe Alley. Farmers there grow **cantaloupes** in great quantities, and the prices for them are much lower on the farm than they'll be in a supermarket. Wherever you find cantaloupes, you'll also find **watermelons.** Seedless watermelons are now making up a larger part of production, and yellow melons are also growing in popularity.

Nuts

The Amish Country really has no nut-producing center, but many people have trees, and you'll find several different kinds of nuts in stores and markets each autumn.

Walnuts and chestnuts have many streets named after them, and walnuts come in two varieties: black and English. The English variety is much more appealing. Chestnut trees once graced much of North America, but a blight a century ago wiped them out. The chestnuts growing today are Chinese chestnuts, an imported variety.

Quite common are horse-chestnut trees, which Longfellow immortalized in his poem, "The Village Blacksmith." The nuts are bitter and inedible, although squirrels certainly like them.

Hickory nuts and filberts also grow in the region, but you'd be very fortunate to find them for sale anywhere.

Roadside Stands

Bring your cooler, or you may be disappointed. As you travel through Lancaster County from May through October, you'll pass roadside stands featuring fruits and vegetables fresh from the fields. If you pack your cooler in the car, you'll be able to arrive at home with all sorts of tasty foods that you know are fresh. Even if you don't bring the cooler, you'll be able to take home many items that will be fine when you get home.

Roadside stands show up in front of many farms, on quiet country roads, and on highways. They sell produce and much more, including baked goods, homemade root beer, and non-food items, such as birdhouses and painted gourds. Look for these stands when you're in the area.

• Route 322 between Ephrata and Blue Ball has a high concentration of stands. This is an excellent place to find cantaloupes, watermelons, and corn.

• The Tomato Barn on Route 999 in Washington Boro sells tomatoes and much more.

• An Amish farm five miles east of Strasburg on Route 741 offers produce, baked goods, and canned goods such as pickles.

• The Corn Wagon on Route 741, just west of Route 324 in New Danville, sells corn at bargain prices.

Restaurants

As Lancaster's population has changed and expanded, so has the variety of flavors available in local restaurants. The Amish and Pennsylvania Dutch restaurants are still dominate, but it's now also possible to enjoy foods from places as diverse as Ireland and Viet Nam in Lancaster.

Pennsylvania Dutch

Amish Barn Restaurant, 3029 Old Philadelphia Pike, **Bird-in-Hand**, (717) 768-8886, www.amishbarnpa.com

Bird-in-Hand Family Restaurant, 2760 Old Philadelphia Pike, **Bird-in-Hand**, (717) 768-8266, www.bird-in-hand.com/restaurant

Family Cupboard Restaurant and Buffet, 3370 Harvest Drive, **Intercourse**, (717) 768-4510

Good N' Plenty Restaurant, Route 896, **Smoketown**, (717) 394-7111, www.goodnplenty.com

Hershey Farm Restaurant and Inn, 240 Hartman Bridge Road, **Ronks**, (717) 687-8635 or (800) 827-8635, www.hersheyfarm.com

The Tomato Barn, Washington Boro

Kreider Farms Restaurant, 1461 Lancaster Road, **Manheim** (717) 665-5039

Leola Family Restaurant, 365 West Main Street, **Leola**, (717) 656-2311, www.bird-in-hand.com/leolarestaurant

Miller's Smorgasbord, 2811 Lincoln Highway East, **Ronks**, (717) 687-6621 or (800) 669-3568, www.millerssmorgasbord.com

Plain and Fancy Farm Restaurant, 3121 Old Philadelphia Pike, **Bird-in-Hand**, (717) 768-4400 or (800) 669-3568, www.plainandfancyfarm.com

Stoltzfus Farm Restaurant, 3716A East Newport Road, **Intercourse**, (717) 768-8156, www.stoltzfusmeats.com

Other Flavors

Belvedere Inn, 402 North Queen Street, **Lancaster**, (717) 394-2422

Cafe Aroma Borealis, 52 North Queen Street, **Lancaster**, (717) 509-9869

Conestoga Restaurant and Bar, 1501 East King Street, **Lancaster**, (717) 393-0290, theconestoga.com

Doneckers Restaurant, 333 North State Street, **Ephrata**, (717) 738-9501, www.doneckers.com

Fred and Mary's Coffee House, 323 West Lemon Street, **Lancaster**, (717) 397-4544

Fulton Bar, 637 North Plum Street, **Lancaster**, (717) 291-1098

General Sutter Inn Restaurant, 14 East Main Street, **Lititz**, (717) 626-2115, www.generalsutterinn.com

Gibraltar Mediterranean Grill, 931 Harrisburg Pike, **Lancaster**, (717) 397-2790

Hall's Cafe, 834 North Plum Street, **Lancaster**, (717) 392-9645

Historic Revere Tavern, 3063 Lincoln Highway East (U.S.

Route 30), **Paradise**, (717) 687-8601 or (800) 429-7383, www.reveretavern.com

Kegel's Seafood Restaurant, 551 West King Street, Lancaster, (717) 397-2832

Lancaster Dispensing Company, 33 North Market Street, Lancaster, (717) 299-4602

Lanvina Vietnamese Restaurants, 1651 Lincoln Highway East, **Lancaster**, (717) 399-0199 and 1762 Columbia Ave., **Lancaster**, 717) 393-7748

Lombardo's Italian American Restaurant, 216 Harrisburg Pike, **Lancaster**, (717) 394-3749, www.lombardosrestaurant.com

Meritage Restaurant, 51 North Market Street, **Lancaster**, (717) 396-1189

Neptune Diner, 924 North Prince Street, **Lancaster**, (717) 399-8358

O'Halloran's Irish Pub, 764 High Street, **Lancaster**, (717) 393-3051

Olde Greenfield Inn, 595 Greenfield Road, **Lancaster**, (717) 393-0668, www.theoldegreenfieldinn.com

Onion's Cafe, 340 North Queen Street, **Lancaster**, (717) 396-8777

Portofino Italian Ristorante, 254 East Frederick Street, **Lancaster**, (717) 394-1635

Pressroom Restaurant, 26-28 West King Street, **Lancaster**, (717) 399-5400, www.pressroomrestaurant.com

Red Rose Luncheonette, 101 East King Street, **Lancaster**, (717) 392-8620

Strawberry Hill, 128 West Strawberry Street, **Lancaster**, (717) 393-5544, www.strawbhill.qpg.com

Taj Mahal, 2080 Bennett Avenue, **Lancaster**, (717) 295-1434

Valentino's Cafe, 132 Rider Avenue, **Lancaster**, (717) 392-9564

Willow Valley Family Restaurant, 2416 Willow Street Pike, **Willow Street**, (717) 464-2711, www.willowvalley.com

Wish You Were Here, 108 West Orange Street, **Lancaster**, (717) 299-5157

Covered Bridges and Active Recreation

The Pennsylvania Dutch Convention and Visitors Bureau does an excellent job of promoting Lancaster County, but the bureau has limitations. Businesses fund the bureau, so it naturally devotes most of its efforts to promoting those businesses. As a result, some great attractions in Lancaster County get less attention than others because they don't have a direct connection to a particular business, even though they have the ability to draw many visitors to the region. The three most prominent categories that meet that criterion are

- covered bridges
- bicycle travel
- the great outdoors

You can certainly get information on these at the bureau, and you can even get directions for a guided bicycle tour that will take you to the three state museums in Lancaster County, but these attractions definitely don't get as much ink as the Amish, shopping, and theatres.

That's good in a way, because it means that you won't encounter the same crowds on a country road as you will at a shopping center.

Covered Bridges
Covered bridges are an important part of Lancaster

County's past and present. Lancaster County leads all Pennsylvania counties in covered bridges still standing and in use, and depending on the criteria used, it's either the number one or number two covered-bridge county in the entire country. (Parke County, Indiana, has more covered bridges than Lancaster County, but Lancaster County has more covered-bridge history than Parke County.)

As of July 2002, Lancaster County had 29 covered bridges standing, with 23 open to traffic. Lancaster County even has a highway crew whose primary responsibility is the maintenance and repair of covered bridges, but unlike other counties with significant numbers of covered bridges, Lancaster County doesn't have a covered-bridge festival or do much to promote its covered bridges. So here's a brief guide to Lancaster County's covered bridges.

The nation's first covered bridge didn't appear in Lancaster County, but it did have a Lancaster connection. Completed in 1805, it spanned the Schuylkill River in Philadelphia and completed the Lancaster Turnpike, the nation's first major road, which linked Philadelphia and Lancaster.

The opening of that bridge began an era of covered-bridge building, and soon they were common throughout Pennsylvania. The longest covered bridge ever built (5,690 feet) spanned the Susquehanna between Columbia in Lancaster County and Wrightsville in York County and opened in 1820. A young lawyer from Lancaster, James Buchanan, served as an attorney for the Columbia Bridge Company, and on October 25, 1820, he submitted an invoice for $77.81.

In 1832, ice washed the bridge away, and its replacement played a role in the Battle of Gettysburg. Confederate soldiers were pursuing Union soldiers east through York County, and when the Union soldiers reached the bridge, they burned it behind them. Subsequently, the Confederates moved back to the west and wound up in the fighting at Gettysburg. By the time of the Civil War, nine of the current covered bridges in Lancaster County were already standing.

Today, Lancaster County residents have a strong attraction to their covered bridges, which helps to explain why Lancaster County has many while neighboring counties have few.

Finding covered bridges can be a challenge. The general rule on the size of them was "a load of hay high and wide," which means that they're generally between ten and 12 feet high and wide enough for only one vehicle. Trucks, buses, and RVs won't fit through a covered bridge, so tour companies can't very well arrange rides through them.

Because of their limitations, covered bridges no longer carry traffic on major roads. Most of them are on country roads that can be difficult to find, but several in Lancaster County are very easy to find. One, in fact, is right beside busy Route 30 along the tourist strip.

Here are four that are easy to locate:

• The Willows—beside Route 30, just west of Route 896 (This is on the grounds of a business, and visitors can drive through it and get out and examine it.)

• Leaman Place—on North Belmont Road, half a mile north of Route 30 in Paradise

• Forry Mill—From Lancaster, go west on Route 23 and pass the traffic light at Prospect Road. Turn right on Bridge Valley Road. The bridge is immediately visible.

• Herr's Mill—on South Ronks Road, two miles south of Route 30 and north of Strasburg (This is on private property and you'll have to pay to see it. If you do, it's good, because you can walk through it and because it's the only two-span bridge left in the county.

Here are two that are less easy to find, but worth the effort:

• Baumgardner Mill—From Lancaster, go south on Route 272 through Willow Street. Immediately after crossing a bridge over the Pequea Creek, turn right on Byerland Church Road. Follow that road several miles to the bridge, and note that the road will change its name to Covered Bridge Road.

Weaverland covered bridge

• Weaverland—At the intersection of Route 23 and Route 322 in Blue Ball, go east on Route 23. Turn north on Route 625. Make the first right on Weaverland Road and go a mile and a half. Follow Weaverland Road when it bends to the left at the intersection with Mill Road. The bridge is half a mile ahead.

Covered bridges are scenic and functional reminders of the past, and they're relatively easy to find in Lancaster County. For more information, contact the Theodore Burr Covered Bridge Society. The society has a book that lists all of the world's covered bridges. P.O. Box 2383, Lancaster, Pennsylvania, 17603-2383, www.tbcbspa.com

The Best Way to Travel—Bicycling

It's possible that God has painted a picture more beautiful than Lancaster County on a pristine summer morning, but if He has, that picture must be hanging in a heavenly gallery, where no earthly mortals can see it.

Verdant fields are bursting with vegetables and fruits. Rows of tall corn tower over fields of melons, beans, squash, pumpkins, tomatoes, potatoes, and just about every other crop that will grow at 40 degrees north latitude. Small orchards offer peaches, plums, and apples. In the fields, parents work beside their children, and on the roads, buggies, bikes, and scooters outnumber cars. At a river crossing, a covered bridge stands as a working reminder of a time when life moved at a slower pace.

On the road, two young Mennonite girls in pastel dresses ride bikes. Coming in the opposite direction are two Mennonite boys on bikes. One has a little trailer hooked to the bike, and he's hauling several boxes of vegetables to the produce auction. At a farm, a stand offers melons, tomatoes, and lots of other goodies directly from fields, but the best part of the stand is the honor system. No one mans the stand, and a box with a hole cut in it serves

First Union Bicycle Race, downtown Lancaster

as the cash register. The expectation is that customers will pay for what they take, and that they'll be able to do enough arithmetic to arrive at the correct price.

The world is a hectic place, but in this little corner of it, tranquility still seems to be doing well. For a visitor, it's easy to fantasize about living in such a world. The reality is that the hard physical work of farm life would be tough to handle, but it's easy to fantasize.

You can see this world through a windshield or a bus window, but on a bicycle, you can be a part of it for a little while. A bike turns a ride through Amish Country into a sensual experience. The sights are much clearer, and so are the smells. On a bike, it's easy to pull to the side of the road to pick a wild raspberry or chat with a horse. On a bike, you can burn off some of those calories that you're sure to consume, and on a bike, it's easy to pull over at a roadside stand for refreshment and replenishment.

Biking through the Amish Country has appeal for everyone. Even if you rarely ride, you can enjoy a few miles on lightly traveled farm roads whose hills are modest. If you're a regular rider, you'll enjoy being able to pedal for miles with minimal interference from cars. Lancaster County natives accept as a birthright the ability to pedal all day on roads with more scenery than cars, but encounters with riders from big cities remind us that we have something special around here. On the third Sunday of every August, the Lancaster Bicycle Club, www.lancasterbikeclub.org, presents its Covered Bridge Metric Century Bike Ride. In 100 kilometers (62 miles) riders pass through seven covered bridges and enjoy lunch at a small town park. For riders who prefer a shorter distance, rides of 50 and 25 kilometers are also available. In addition, the club has rides every week, when the weather permits.

Dream Ride Cycling hosts bicycling on many levels. The most infamous is the Nightmare Ride, held the second Saturday in June. It takes riders on a grueling, one day, 177-mile jaunt around the perimeter of Lancaster County. The ride is always hilly, and it's usually hot, but many people complete it.

Somewhat less difficult are the Dream Rides held the following week. They offer rides of 15, 30, 62, and 100 miles around the farmlands of Lancaster County.

Dream Rides also offers guided tours at a pace that suits the rider's ability. One tour option includes lodging in a bed and breakfast. For more information, call (717) 397-2503 or check the Web site at www.dreamrideprojects.org.

Two Fun Rides

• **Strasburg RailRoad Route**—This is about ten miles of easy terrain from Strasburg to Paradise and back. Route 741, where the ride begins and ends, is busy, but the rest of the roads have little traffic.

Begin at the Railroad Museum of Pennsylvania.

Go east on Route 741.

Turn left on Esbenshade Road.

Turn left on Cherry Hill Road.

Turn right on Oak Hill Road.

Turn left on Black Horse Road.

Turn right on Oak Hill Road.

Turn right on Tiffany Avenue.

What You'll See: At the end of the ride you'll be able to see trains from the Strasburg RailRoad turning around. Along the route, you'll see many Amish farms. It's a short, pleasant ride.

• **Mennonite Country—New Holland to Terre Hill**

This is a pleasant ride on roads with low traffic. The only decent hill takes you into Terre Hill. This ride also works well in a car.

Begin at New Holland Community Park. (It's on Jackson Street on the eastern side of town. To reach it from Route 23, turn south on South Kinzer Avenue. The park is right beside the railroad tracks.)

Go north on Kinzer Avenue.

Turn right on Spruce Street and quickly left on Reidenbach Road.

Turn right on Martin Road.
Cross Route 322 with caution.
Turn left on White Oak Road.
Turn right on Lancaster Avenue.
Turn right into Terre Hill Memorial Park. (To spot it, look to your right as you enter the park. It's in a little gully, below the picnic area.)
Continue through the park.
Turn right on Main Street.
Turn right on PA 897.
Turn right on Long Lane.
Turn right on Martindale Road.
Turn left White Oak Road.
Turn right on Conestoga Avenue.
Turn left on Gristmill Road.
Cross Route 322 with caution.
Turn left on Shirk Road.
Turn left on Huyard Road.
Turn right on Reidenbach Road.
Turn right on Spruce Street.
Turn left on Kinzer Avenue.
Cross Route 23 and return to the park.

What You'll See: At the corner of Lancaster Avenue and Quarry Road is a one-room Mennonite school. Usually, the students leave their bikes lying on the grass outside the school. Terre Hill Memorial Park has restrooms, a great view, and a hidden covered bridge.

The Great Outdoors

Lancaster County doesn't have a reputation as a place to enjoy the woods and waters, but a lightly promoted fact is that the county actually has many outstanding areas for hiking, bird-watching, camping, and boating.

The Susquehanna River is the entire western border of Lancaster County, and the river is very popular with boaters.

The river is shallow and rocky, and it doesn't have any ships on it, but it's fine for pleasure boats, at least little ones.

If you don't have a boat with you, you can still enjoy the river. The area along the river is much hillier and more rugged than the agricultural heart of Lancaster County. A state park, wildflower preserves, and great places to sit and watch the water flow are available all along the river. From north to south, here are some of the best places to enjoy the wide Susquehanna River:

• **Conoy Canal Park** is accessible from Collins Road off Route 441. The park extends over a mile and has a boat access.

• **Chickies Rock County Park** lies between Columbia and Marietta along route 441. It has hiking trails and great views of the river.

• **Washington Boro Park,** at the intersection of routes 441 and 999, is a good place to have a picnic and watch the river go by.

• **Safe Harbor Park** lies at the confluence of the Conestoga River and the Susquehanna.

• **Tucquan Glen Nature Preserve** is a wild area that borders the river and is accessible from River Road.

• **Muddy Run Recreation Area** is the place with the best facilities near the river. It has areas for tents.

• **Susquehannock State Park** is a small natural area adjacent to Muddy Run. The park offers great views of the river and many islands, including Mt. Johnson Island, which was the first piece of land set aside in the world as a bald eagle sanctuary. Eagles and other birds of prey, such as osprey and hawks, are often visible along the river.

The park has five miles of scenic hiking trails. Holly, rhododendron, and wildflowers fill the trails with color, and deer and other wildlife are common sights.

• The river region is an area that few visitors to Lancaster County see. One good way to see it is to drive along River Road, which extends from the Dauphin County border near

Three Mile Island to Muddy Run Recreation Area. North of Route 999, River Road is Route 441.

Away from the river, Lancaster County has some other interesting outdoor areas. At the top of the list is **Middle Creek Wildlife Management Area.** Covering several thousand acres in northern Lancaster County and southern Lebanon County, Middle Creek is home to birds of all sorts, and visitors come to watch Canada geese, eagles, bluebirds, wild turkeys, and even the turkey vultures that sit on the power lines.

In spring, flocks of snow geese are so large that they can make hillsides appear to be covered with snow when they're actually covered with birds. For hikers, the area offers miles of trails, including the Horseshoe Trail. The visitors center explains everything that's available. To reach Middle Creek from Lancaster, go north on Route 501. Go east on Route 322. Turn left on Hopeland Road, which is at the bottom of a long hill in the village of Clay. Turn right at the stop sign. Turn left on Kleinfeltersville Road, and it will take you into Middle Creek Wildlife Management Area.

• **Lancaster County Central Park** lies partially within the city of Lancaster, and it's a popular place with trail runners and hikers. Miles of trails wind through the park, and it's not uncommon to see deer and blue herons within city limits. To reach the park from downtown Lancaster, go south on Duke Street. Turn right on Chesapeake Street, and at the bottom of the hill, turn left into the park.

• **Money Rocks Park** is a largely undeveloped wooded area with some hiking trails. Narvon Road, Narvon

Running

If you enjoy running, you'll find a good collection of races in Lancaster County, as well as quiet country roads and wooded trails on which you can run for fun.

The two biggest races in the county are
• Race against Racism (5K) last Saturday in April

• Red Rose Run (5 miles) first Saturday in June
Both take place in downtown Lancaster.

Some other good races are

• Mrs. Smith's Challenge—5 miles on trails, women only, day before Mother's Day

• Smith's Challenge—10K or 20K on trails, men only, Father's Day

• Run for Peace—5K or 10K, Elizabethtown, late June

• Firecracker—5 miles, Ephrata, July 4

• Shoo-fly—5 miles, Terre Hill, July, in conjunction with Terre Hill Days

• Blue Ball—5 miles, Saturday before Labor Day

Blue Ball 5-Miler

Blue heron, Middle Creek Wildlife Management Area

Covered bridge at Willow Valley Resort (pedestrians only)

- Lancaster Family YMCA Triathlon—Speedwell Forge Lake, Saturday after Labor Day
- Conestoga Trail Run—10 miles, Pequea, last Sunday in September
- Mount Hope Distance Classic—7 miles, Mount Hope Winery, Manheim, last Saturday in October

For information on the local running scene, visit the Lancaster Road Runners Club's Web site at www.geocities.com/lrrclub.

Golfing

Lancaster County has many public golf courses. Some are part of a program called Capital Region Golf, which offers packages and discounts for courses in Lancaster, York, Harrisburg, and the surrounding areas. For details, call (800) 942-2444.

The most unusual course in the area is Iron Valley. It occupies a site that was once the largest iron-ore mine east of the Mississippi. The course features lots of trees, lots of water, and steep elevation changes.

Iron Valley Golf Club, Route 322, **Cornwall**, (717) 279-7409, www.ironvalley.com

Crossgates Golf Course, One Crossland Pass, **Millersville**, (717) 872-4500, www.crossgatesgolf.com

Hawk Valley Golf Course, 1319 Crestview Drive, **Denver**, (717) 445-5445 or (800) 522-HAWK, www.golfthehawk.com

Lancaster Host Golf Resort, 2300 Lincoln Highway East, **Lancaster**, (717) 299-5500 or (800) 233- 0121, www.lancaster-host.com

Tanglewood Manor Golf Club, 653 Scotland Road, **Quarryville**, (717) 786-2220, www.twgolf.com

Tree Top Golf Course, 1624 Creek Road, **Manheim**, (717) 665-6262, www.treetopgolf.com

Willow Valley Resort Golf Course, 2416 Willow Street Pike, **Lancaster**, (717) 464-4448 or (800) 444-1714, www.willowvalley.com

Calendar

Winter is definitely the slow time in Pennsylvania. Once spring arrives, the activity level picks up and continues through the Christmas season. Summer and autumn are full of festivals, fairs, and celebrations.

January

Pork and Sauerkraut Dinner, New Year's Day, Leola Fire Company, Route 23, Leola

Pennsylvania Farm Show, second week of the month, State Farm Show Building, Harrisburg. Unlike most other states, which hold their state fairs during warmer months, Pennsylvania has its show in January, and tradition says that the worst weather of the year accompanies the farm show.

February

Groundhog Day, February 2. The big attention goes to Punxsutawney Phil in northwestern Pennsylvania, but Lancaster County has Octorara Orphie. Every February 2 he emerges from his burrow and predicts the weather for the next six weeks.

Fasnacht Day, Tuesday before the first day of Lent. Bakeries throughout Pennsylvania Dutch Country produce fasnachts

133

(doughnuts) as a final splurge before the self-denial of the Lenten season. On Fasnacht Day, fasnachts are available in markets, stores, and restaurants throughout the region.

March

Gordonville Fire Company Auction, second Saturday, (717) 768-3869. The most famous of the mud sales offers quilts, handcrafts, farm equipment, and much more to raise money for the volunteer fire company.

Charter Day, for state museums, second Sunday. Admission is free at Landis Valley Farm Museum, Railroad Museum of Pennsylvania, Ephrata Cloister, Cornwall Iron Furnace, and all state museums.

Spring planting begins.

April

Quilters' Heritage Celebration, first week of April, Lancaster Host Resort and Conference Center, 2300 Lincoln Highway East, Lancaster, (717) 299-5500

Art Walk, last weekend, downtown Lancaster

Race against Racism, 5K, last Saturday, Musser Park, downtown Lancaster, (717) 291-4758

May

Loyalty Day Parade, first Saturday, downtown Lancaster

Lancaster Spring Show of Arts and Crafts, first weekend, Lancaster County Central Park, (717) 295-1500

Spring Steam-Up, second weekend, Rough and Tumble Museum, Route 30, Kinzers, (717) 442-4249

Opening Day at **Dutch Wonderland** and **HersheyPark,** second weekend, (800) HERSHEY, www.dutchwonderland.com

Rhubarb Festival, third Saturday, Kitchen Kettle Village, Intercourse, (800) 732-3538

Riverside Craft Days, Memorial Day weekend, John Wright Mansion, Wrightsville, (717) 252-2519

June

First Union Bike Race—downtown Lancaster, first Tuesday, (717) 291-4758. Cyclists who will compete in America's biggest one-day race in Philadelphia the following Sunday compete in Lancaster on Tuesday.

Red Rose 5-Mile Race, downtown Lancaster, first Saturday, (717) 291-4758

Landis Valley Fair, Landis Valley Farm Museum, first Saturday, (717) 569-0401

Woodcarving Show, first Saturday, Kitchen Kettle Village, Intercourse, (800) 732-3538

Smith's Challenge, 10K and 20K trail races, Lancaster County Central Park, Father's Day

First local tomatoes and corn arrive.

July

Civil War Reenactment, weekend preceeding or including July 4, Gettysburg Battlefield

July 4 Celebration and fireworks, downtown Lancaster, Friday before July 4, (717) 291-4758

Old-Fashioned Fourth, Musser Park, downtown Lancaster

Firecracker 5-Mile Race, Ephrata, July 4

Terre Hill Days, town festival featuring Shoo-fly 5-Mile Race, second or third weekend

Ice-Cream Festival, third Sunday, downtown Lancaster, (717) 291-4758

Pennsylvania State Craft Show and Sale, last Thursday through Sunday, Franklin and Marshall College

Lititz Outdoor Art Show, last Saturday, downtown Lititz, (717) 626-8981

August

Fiddlers' Picnic, first Sunday, Lancaster County Central Park, (717) 299-8215

Lancaster Fest, second Saturday, downtown Lancaster, street fair featuring food and music, (717) 291-4758

Heritage Day, second Saturday, Hans Herr House, Willow Street, (717) 464-4438

Covered Bridge Metric Century Bike Ride, www.lancasterbike-club.org, 100K course takes cyclists through seven covered bridges.

Mount Gretna Outdoor Art Show, third Saturday

September

Blue Ball 5-Mile Race, Saturday of Labor Day weekend, 8 A.M., East Earl Township Office, Route 322

Long's Park Arts and Crafts Festival, Labor Day weekend, (717) 295-7054, info@longspark.org, or www.longspark.org

Labor Day Auction, (717) 295-3900, Lampeter Fairgrounds, Route 741 in Lampeter, benefits Hospice of Lancaster County, Chadds Ford, Pennsylvania

Strasburg Heritage Day, Saturday after Labor Day, (717) 687-6878, annual antique and craft fair

Lancaster Family YMCA Triathlon, 1.5K swim, 40K bike, 10K run, Saturday after Labor Day, Speedwell Forge Lake, Lititz, (717) 394-7474

Annual Mushroom Festival, weekend after Labor Day, Kennett Square, (888) 440-9920, www.mushroomfest.com

Wheels, Wheels, Wheels, downtown Lancaster, Sunday after

Labor Day. The streets of downtown Lancaster host a Classic Car and Cycle Show, (717) 291-4758.

Middle Creek Wildfowl Show, third weekend, Middle Creek Visitor Center, (717) 733-1512

Puerto Rican Parade, third Saturday, downtown Lancaster, (717) 291-4758

Eastern Primitive Rendezvous, third weekend, Muddy Run Park, Holtwood, (717) 284-4325

Architectural History Tour/Historic Preservation, fourth Sunday, (717) 291-5861

Antiques Extravaganza, last weekend, Adamstown, (717) 738-9010

Annual Gordonville Fire Company Fall Quilt Auction, last Saturday, (717) 768-3869, Gordonville Fire Company, 3204 Vigilant Street, Gordonville

October

Autumn's Colors at Longwood Gardens, (610) 388-1000, www.longwoodgardens.org, U.S. Route 1, Kennett Square

Bridge Bust, Wrightsville/Columbia, first Saturday, (717) 684-5249. The mile-long Veteran's Memorial Bridge (PA 462) closes to traffic and becomes the site of a festival.

JazzFest, Art Sunday and Outdoor Restaurant Fair, first Sunday, downtown Lancaster, (717) 291-4758

Harvest Days, Landis Valley Museum, second weekend, (717) 569-0401

Lancaster Town Fair, downtown Lancaster, a Wednesday and Thursday in mid-October, (717) 393-1735. Two days of arts, crafts, antiques, food, exhibits, and events at churches and other institutions.

Pumpkin Patch at Landis Valley Museum, last weekend, (717) 569-0401

November

Christmas in Hershey, mid-month through Christmas, (800) HERSHEY

A Dickens Christmas, weekends late November through December, Mount Hope Winery, PA 72 and Pennsylvania Turnpike, (717) 665-7021

Savor the Season, late November through December, Kitchen Kettle Village, Intercourse, (800) 732-3538

December

Tuba Christmas, first Friday in December, downtown Lancaster, (717) 291-4758. Carolers sing to music provided by dozens of tubas.

Victorian Christmas, early in the month, Wheatland, (717) 392-8721

Bird-in-Hand Celebration of Lights, weekends in December, (717) 768-8272. Event features thousands of lights, holiday music, and other special events.

Santa Trains, the two weekends before Christmas, Strasburg RailRoad, (717) 687-7522 or www.strasburgrailroad.com

Countdown Lancaster, December 31, New Year's Eve celebration in downtown Lancaster, (717) 291-4758

Index

A